"To understand and address the many issues of our cultural moment, from abortion to racial injustice, we've got to start with the *imago Dei*. *The Dignity Revolution* helps us recover this biblical concept, pushing and pleading with us to apply it constantly and consistently."

Matt Chandler, Lead Pastor of Teaching, the Village Church, Flower Mound, Texas; President, Acts29; Author, *Take Heart*

"For years I thought that only the lives of elderly and medically fragile people were under assault—it's what happens in a culture that insists you are 'better off dead than disabled.' Now, however, the human dignity of families living on every cul-de-sac in America is under attack as the very definition of 'human being' is altered. No longer is this an academic issue; its impact is creeping into hospitals, schools, and businesses and our country is reeling. Daniel Darling's new book *The Dignity Revolution* is a must-read for every Christian looking for a solid language and good argument to halt the further dismantling of the sanctity of all human life. I highly recommend it!"

Joni Eareckson Tada, Joni and Friends International Disability Center

"We need a revolution in our country of committed followers of Jesus who are consistently living out the value of human dignity in how we speak, act, think, and relate to one another. I'm grateful this timely book offers us a way forward in having a consistent pro-life public witness that will have enduring impact on the church and society at large."

Jenny Yang, Vice President of Advocacy and Policy, World Relief

"Twenty-five years from now, if evangelical Christians are known for their promotion of human dignity, their love of neighbor, and their commitment to justice and mercy, the compelling vision of Dan Darling's *The Dignity Revolution* will be the reason why. This book belongs on the bookshelf of every serious American Christian."

Bruce Ashford, Provost, Southeastern Baptist Theological Seminary

"Americans are longing for a vision of politics and public life that is grounded in principle, not partisanship, and Christianity demands such a vision. My friend Dan Darling offers such a vision here, grounded in the dignity of each and every human being as made in the image of God. Consider this book carefully, and then act to implement its vision in your personal and public life."

Michael Wear, Author, *Reclaiming Hope: Lessons Learned in the Obama White House About the Future of Faith in America*

"The kingdom of God redefines for us who matters and what matters. Human beings are not the sum of their physical, economic, and mental powers. We are creatures who reflect, all of us, a picture of the Creator God. I know of no one who cares for human dignity more than my friend and colleague Daniel Darling. This book appeals to the imagination and the conscience about what it would look like were we to treat our neighbors, and ourselves, as created in the image of God."

Russell Moore, President, the Ethics and Religious Liberty Commission; Author, *Onward*

"*The Dignity Revolution* is a terrific introduction to thinking Christianly about pressing social issues of our day, including abortion and euthanasia, race and immigration, poverty and justice systems, sexuality and marriage. If you or your millennial children are wondering whether evangelicals in the public sphere have anything to offer besides interest-group politics, read this book."

Dr. Marvin Olasky, Editor-in-chief, *World Magazine*

"If there's a revolution I'd like to join, it's this one! God calls us to love our neighbor as ourselves—and Dan Darling's book will assist us in that commandment. *The Dignity Revolution* will equip, challenge, and inspire readers to see people as God does. Thank you, Dan, for writing this timeless and important book—may we all have ears to hear."

Trillia Newbell, Author, *United* and *God's Very Good Idea*

"The spirit of the day has proclaimed itself compassionate while failing to recognize the dignity of every person in every condition, under every circumstance. *The Dignity Revolution* details how the Christian doctrine of human dignity must guide our public engagement. Darling compels us not to be merely pious bystanders, but also vigilant servants determined to put our convictions into action on issues such as criminal justice, immigration, and religious liberty."

Justin E. Giboney, President, the AND Campaign

"This may be one of the most important books of our time. This isn't a book to merely be read—this is an igniting catalyst of a desperately needed revolution that could turn everything around for every single one of us and this whole brokenhearted world."

Ann Voskamp, *New York Times* bestselling author, *One Thousand Gifts*

"This book should be on the shelf of anyone wanting to seriously engage the most difficult topics and conversations of our day. Not only will it inform and equip you, but it will give you confidence in how Christians should respond to society's most difficult conversations."

Gabe Lyons, Founder, Q Forum; Author,
unChristian and *The Next Christians*

"We live in an age of mass confusion about what it means to be human. Our dignity is repeatedly attacked by new worldviews which undermine the significance of human beings. This book is a compelling and careful articulation of human dignity according to Scripture. *The Dignity Revolution* carefully traces the worth of human endeavors and articulates a compelling vision for what it means to bear God's image. Darling is a faithful guide on these issues and this book is a welcome resource for the church."

Dr. Albert Mohler, President, the Southern Baptist
Theological Seminary

"Daniel Darling has provided us with an accessible, faithful, understanding, Christ-centered guide to some of the most pressing ethical issues facing us today. Our God-given dignity is good news for each one of us, and this book shows us why."

Sam Allberry, speaker for Ravi Zacharias International Ministries;
Author, *Is God Anti-Gay?* and *Seven Myths About Singleness*

"In our current 'hashtag age'—where virtues such as kindness, civility, and love are in decline—a new vocabulary and tone around the glory and worth of all persons is sorely needed. In this helpful volume, Daniel does a lovely job of championing such a vocabulary and tone. I commend *The Dignity Revolution* to you… it will be well worth your time."

Scott Sauls, Senior Pastor, Christ Presbyterian Church, Nashville,
Tennessee; Author, *Jesus Outside the Lines* and *Befriend*

"You would think that by now we would appreciate the value of these two words: human dignity. But the daily news reminds us otherwise. And Dan Darling reminds us of the urgency of understanding the phrase in its rich biblical dimensions, and, most importantly, of living out the reality that every person on the planet is of immense value."

Mark Galli, Editor-in-chief, *Christianity Today*

"I think most Christians could tell you that humans are made *imago Dei*—in God's image and likeness—but I don't think many fully grasp what that means or how to apply this fundamental idea to our most pressing cultural concerns. This is tragic, because it is precisely here that Christians have so much to offer a confused world right now. This book is overdue and crucial, and should be required reading for all of us."

John Stonestreet, President, the Colson Center
for Christian Worldview

"The most important question of contemporary ethics, and perhaps of culture itself, is whether the dignity of the person can be grounded in something other than arbitrary exertions of power. Significantly, this question arises at a time of unprecedented frustration with a binary left/right political imagination left over from the culture-war fought by my students' grandparents. Darling's book shows how Christians can avoid the idolatry of left/right-style secular politics, while beautifully grounding the dignity of the person in ways which can claim the conscience of the Christian and attract the attention of the curious non-believer."

Charlie Camosy, Associate Professor of Theological and Social
Ethics, Fordham University; Board Member, Democrats for Life

"Across all spectrums, human dignity is a flag Christians wave. It is central to our identity and mission. Standing athwart our polarized age, *The Dignity Revolution* points to the common ground we share and the broader mission we pursue."

Chris Horst, Vice President, Hope International

"The journey of life is the story of people bearing the image of God. With the gospel always present, Dan Darling challenges us in *The Dignity Revolution* to see the many roads human dignity travels, and to consider how consistent we are in respecting the sacred image God created us to possess. It is a challenge well worth taking on as we seek to reflect and honor God with how we live as Christians."

Darrell Bock, Executive Director for Cultural Engagement,
Howard G. Hendricks Center

"For many Christians, today's politics is deeply unsatisfying. One side cares about the unborn, but not about refugees. The other side cares about immigrants, but not the unborn child. Daniel Darling is leading a quiet revolution that transcends the old left-versus-right paradigm and, instead, summons us to consistently defend human dignity."

Matt K. Lewis, Senior Columnist, *The Daily Beast*;
CNN Political Commentator

DANIEL DARLING

THE DIGNITY REVOLUTION

RECLAIMING GOD'S RICH
VISION FOR HUMANITY

thegoodbook
COMPANY

This book is dedicated to the most vulnerable among us,
in places nobody sees,
ignored by the masses of people walking by,
ignorant of their plight.

God, who formed you in his image,
sees you and loves you.

The Dignity Revolution: Reclaiming the Bible's Rich Vision for Humanity
© Daniel Darling, 2018.

Published by:
The Good Book Company

Email (US): info@thegoodbook.com
Email (UK): info@thegoodbook.co.uk

Websites:
North America: www.thegoodbook.com
UK: www.thegoodbook.co.uk
Australia: www.thegoodbook.com.au
New Zealand: www.thegoodbook.co.nz

ISBN: 9781784982836 | Printed in the UK

Design by André Parker

CONTENTS

FOREWORD

Every year, *Forbes* magazine releases a list of the world's billionaires—uber-wealthy people ranked by their net worth. When someone soars to the top due to a lucrative sale or stock spike, it makes headlines. News about the rich getting richer is clickbait in our culture.

Wealth is a primary measure of worth in the West, but there are others: celebrity status, physical beauty, political power, athletic accomplishments, citizenship, social-media influence. We live in a world that places price tags on people. Wealthy, successful, powerful people are highly valued. Poor, homeless, powerless people are not.

God's people don't see these price tags, right? If that were so, Dan Darling wouldn't need to write this book. But it isn't so. Basic human dignity is floundering in our status-seeking, increasingly nationalistic world, and Christians are not immune.

Stereotyping people in ways that diminish them is, of course, nothing new; it has happened throughout history, resulting in the Holocaust, the enslavement of Africans, the internment of Japanese Americans, racial segregation, the Rwandan genocide, the systematic oppression of women… I could go on. In all of these injustices, the church was often either complicit or perhaps just looked the other way.

And what about today? In a recent survey by Barna Research, when Americans were asked if people from other countries enriched our culture, evangelicals were the least likely of the demographic groups to agree.[1] On the question of whether America should accept refugees in their time of crisis, evangelicals were the least welcoming of all groups, with just 16 percent saying yes.

Clearly this calls for some soul-searching.

CHANGING THE PRICE TAGS

As Christ-followers, we can find our most powerful teaching on human dignity and worth in the life and example of Jesus.

Jesus' actions and associations challenged the status quo and spoke to the value of all people. His inner circle was a motley crew of simple fishermen, a zealot, a tax collector, and women (a cultural and religious taboo). He healed and touched people with skin diseases, lifelong disabilities, and demon possession. He publicly interacted with Samaritans and sinners. And the first person to join him in paradise was a convicted felon—the thief on the cross.

Again and again, Jesus loved the unlovable, touched the untouchable, valued the undervalued, and welcomed the unwanted. He changed the price tags. He crossed out the paltry prices that had been assigned to these people and replaced them with one word: PRICELESS. He saw people as not just worthy of some simple kindness, but so precious that he would pay the ultimate price for each one of them.

Of all Jesus' interactions with the sick and the sinful, I find the brief story of the healing of a leper in Mark chapter 1 most instructive for our times. Mark 1 v 40-42 reads:

> *A man with leprosy came and knelt in front of Jesus, begging to be healed. "If you are willing, you can heal me and make me clean," he said. Moved with compassion, Jesus reached out and touched him. "I am willing," he said. "Be*

---

1 barna.com/research/americans-soften-immigration-2017/. Accessed 5/2/18.

healed!" Instantly the leprosy disappeared, and the man was healed. (New Living Translation)

Jesus' unexpected actions provide three takeaways for us. First, Jesus interacts with this man of the lowest status in society—a person not just diseased and disfigured but untouchable, according to Jewish law and Roman custom. No other religious or civic leader would have stopped to interact with such a person. Jesus was making a clear statement: *Every person—every life—is precious to God.*

Second, we read that Jesus was moved with compassion—not filled with fear, disgust, or judgment. Nor was he influenced by the Pharisees or the political climate. The takeaway for us: *We need to react to all people—especially the marginalized—with love and compassion.*

Third, Jesus not only touched this man—a man who perhaps had not felt a human touch for years—but he saw his pain and said, "I am willing. Be healed." He not only saw and sympathized with this man who was deemed worthless; he also acted. The lesson for us: *Jesus calls us to reach into the pain and brokenness of our world.* He wants his people to be like firefighters—rushing toward the fire of human suffering instead of away from it.

So who are the lepers today? Be honest with yourself. Are there groups of people whose worth you have, in your perspective of them, reduced or discounted? Refugees, Muslims, undocumented immigrants, people with AIDS, those on welfare, the homeless? More and more, it's common to devalue people on ideological grounds: If you're conservative, you reject liberals; if you're in favor of gun control, you vilify gun owners. When we look at other human beings through the distorting lenses of culture, politics, patriotism, and fear, we fail to see them as God does—made in his own image and of priceless value.

Through God's eyes, all people are fearfully and wonderfully made—precious in his sight. As followers of Jesus Christ, this is the view of humanity we must embrace, so that we respond with compassion to the brokenness in our communities and our world.

Dan's book is timely as we navigate a divisive, politicized climate, both in the US and throughout the Western world. It's imperative now that those of us who follow Jesus reaffirm our biblical vision of human dignity in the face of confusing public discourse. Titling this book a "Dignity Revolution" is no overstatement, for Jesus called us to take the world by storm, like revolutionaries, and to value every human life as priceless. This is what attracted people to Jesus during his time on earth, and it still draws people today.

We will never win the world for Christ if we fail to demonstrate his unconditional love for all people. As the apostle Paul said in 2 Corinthians 5 v 20, "We are therefore Christ's ambassadors, as though God were making his appeal through us" (NLT).

Richard Stearns, President of World Vision U.S.
and the author of "The Hole in Our Gospel"

INTRODUCTION
A PERSON'S A PERSON

It was a weekday morning and we packed our four kids into the minivan and rambled down Route 40 toward that venerable Nashville landmark The Grand Ole Opry. We weren't there to see one of our favorite country music artists, but a live production of Dr. Seuss's *Horton Hears a Who*.

To be honest, while the rest of the family was excited, I admit that if my wife hadn't politely asked (ordered) me to take a day off work, I wouldn't have made this entertainment choice. So as we settled into our comfortable chairs at the Opry, I prepared myself to be bored. I thoroughly enjoy theater, but I had low expectations for a production designed to amuse children and, by extension, weary adults. I consoled myself with a fully-charged iPhone, invented for these kinds of situations. My plan was to dim the brightness, read a few online articles I'd bookmarked on my browser, and re-emerge after the play.

I never looked at my iPhone.

I was enraptured by the performance. I'd read the book a few times as a kid and a few more as a parent, but it wasn't until I saw Dr. Seuss's vivid morality tale on stage, under the lights, that its powerful, repeated message grabbed my heart:

"A person's a person, no matter how small."

When I heard this phrase, I sat straight up. It was so simple, so obvious, and so compelling. "Yes," I thought, "every person really is a… person, no matter what their usefulness to society, no matter how seemingly insignificant they are, no matter what their stature."

A person's a person. What a thought for our strange and confused age.

DR. SEUSS AND THE A-BOMB

Curious, I researched (later, of course, with my iPhone firmly in my pocket) the origins of *Horton Hears a Who.* I discovered that Theodore Geisel, aka Dr. Seuss, wrote this children's book after he took a tour of Japan in 1953. It was an eye-opening journey for the author. During World War II, Geisel had used his creative gifts to rally America to the Allied cause. His pro-America cartoons were a fixture in newspapers and magazines across the country. Geisel was a steadfast supporter of President Franklin Roosevelt and the fight for freedom against the fascism of Germany, Japan, and Italy.

But Geisel's work went beyond patriotism. In his cartoons, he presented Japanese people as less than human. His illustrations helped stoke an ugly anti-Japanese sentiment in the US, at a time when Japanese-Americans were ordered to evacuate their homes and were interned in camps. I googled some of his old wartime images and was shocked at the way his work dehumanized Japanese Americans. Geisel's work was tinder for the fires of racial resentment. But when the artist visited Japan and met survivors of the devastating atomic bombs that rained down on Nagasaki and Hiroshima, on many tens of thousands of Japanese people, something changed inside him. He saw humanity in people he had once considered subhuman.

And so, when he returned to America, Geisel apologized

in the clearest way he knew how. He wrote a children's book: *Horton Hears a Who.*

Though he was raised Lutheran, there isn't much in Geisel's life to indicate genuine faith in Christ. The ethic he presented in Horton, however, borrows from the beautiful Christian idea that every single human life has dignity. This was what Geisel had come to realize, too late for him to un-draw his cartoons but not too late for him to write this signature line in his book: a person's a person, no matter how small.

RECOVERING DIGNITY

The easy temptation for us is to look back at Theodore Geisel's time and assume we'd behave differently. We know (don't we?) not to dehumanize a whole group of people. We like to write ourselves into history as the heroes, and assure ourselves that we have learned from past mistakes.

But let's not do that too fast. It's always easier to see the blindspots of another culture, and another political position, and another's heart, than it is our own. About what might our grandchildren wonder how we could ever have thought as we do, or lived as we do, or kept quiet as we do?

The truth is that we live in a world of terrible, daily assaults on humans, from war to famine to sexual assault to poverty, from the earliest stages of life to the last. And we're tempted, like people in every era but perhaps more so today, to let our tribal affiliations and cultural prejudices blind us to real human tragedy or, worse, be complicit in the marginalizing of people groups. What's more, advances in technology are challenging our assumptions about what it means to be human.

We need a fresh approach to engaging with the world. I'd like to suggest that this can be found in a recovery of the robust Christian doctrine of human dignity.

Imagine, for a moment, if God's people began to lead a new, quiet revolution whose foundation was a simple premise: every human being—no matter who they are, no matter where they are, no matter what they have done or have had done to them—possesses dignity, because every human being is created in the image of God. By God's grace, our churches would change, and our communities would change.

MAKE A DIFFERENCE

This book is for you if you find yourself without any home in the political parties of your nation. It's for you if deep down you feel your positions on important issues are increasingly being shaped not by biblical convictions but by political allegiance. It's for you if you'd like to be involved in helping those who seem vulnerable, or struggling, or broken, but you don't know what to do, or how to do it, or whether it would really make a difference anyway—or you just never get around to it when there's so much else to do.

As you read, at times you will feel validated, and at times you will feel uncomfortable. This is as it should be, for none of God's people are yet perfect, and all of God's people are "sojourners and exiles" till Christ returns to renew and restore all things (1 Peter 2 v 11). But while we await Jesus' coming, we are invited to participate in his mission—to make a difference while we wait. We're to witness to where we're heading and to whom we're heading.

We need a renewed way of interacting with and speaking to the world. We need a human-dignity movement.

This is about more than simple compassion. Human dignity must be at the heart of our Christian lives because it is at the heart of the gospel story. The gospel celebrates a God who both created humanity with purpose and who—when that humanity turned their back on their Creator—rescued humanity through his Son, the divine human

Jesus, in order to recreate and repurpose them. Jesus cared enough about humanity to become a human. The Spirit cares enough about humanity to transform us as humans. And when we ascribe the value to humanity—all humanity—that Jesus did and does, we realize that part of living as a Christian and part of believing as a Christian is to view people the way God views them.

A gospel-saturated human dignity movement unites two seemingly disparate strands of the Christian life. It reminds us that personal salvation without neighbor love is an incomplete gospel, and it reminds us that social justice without individual transformation is powerless. Human dignity is simple, it's compelling… and it's often been ignored. Human dignity is often assumed or downplayed in our books and in our preaching and in our thinking. But part of living as a Christian, part of believing as a Christian, is to view others, and ourselves, as possessing far greater dignity than we naturally think, and to live in a way that is consistent with that view.

This book is not about left or right. It's about seeing the people of the world the way God sees them. This is a book that imagines what it would look like and how our societies could flourish if we moved beyond our intransigent tribal politics or increasingly weary apathy and worked to create societies that are good for our neighbors—all our neighbors. It isn't exhaustive—I haven't included every single area where looking at others in this way makes a difference. But this book will show you what happens in us and what can happen through us if we really do see that a person's a person, no matter how small, or different, or distant.

DO SOMETHING

I'm writing this book not simply for thought leaders and power brokers (though I hope they do read it!). I am writing for everyday Christians: the faithful followers of Jesus around the world who seek to live their lives, every day, on mission for God. If we're to be faithful stewards in this age in which God has placed us, I'm convinced that we must each understand what it really means to be truly human.

I believe the church is the most powerful institution in the world, the most powerful catalyst for social change, with the most powerful message in existence, because the church is the place where God's Spirit most powerfully dwells. So this book is for pastors and plumbers, columnists and craftsmen, mayors and moms. It's for CEOs and Sunday-school teachers, accountants and astronauts, dynamic speakers and day laborers.

And it's calling us to be engaged.

Remember Theodore Geisel? On his visit to Japan, his eyes were opened to the basic humanity of the people of that country. And on his return to the US, he did something about it. He did what he could. He wrote a kids' book.

God is calling all of us not just to see that people have dignity, but to act accordingly. Not just to know, but to do.

To be fully captured by the Bible's rich vision of human dignity will provoke us to act in different ways. Some will feel the call to run for office... others will roll up their sleeves and join the good work of nonprofit ministry... and others might simply find little ways to incorporate this vision of human dignity into their everyday lives and change their community one word, one action, one person at a time. Each one of us can be, and are called to be, part of this movement—a human dignity revolution that our societies need, and that we—you—are uniquely placed as Christians to join.

Because a person's a person, no matter how small.

1. WITH GLORY AND HONOR

"A feature of the dignity that accrues to us by virtue of our being destined for fellowship with God is that no actual humiliation that might befall us can extinguish it."

WOLFHART PANNENBERG

What exactly does it mean to be human? And what does it mean to see the humanity of others?

Regardless of your religious or moral framework, there is an instinctive sense within each of our hearts that whispers the truth to us that being human matters.

Consider, for instance, our reaction to death. Why do we recoil when we learn of another mass shooting, another terrorist attack, or another natural disaster? Why do we feel deep pain when someone we love is lost to cancer or some other disease? Why do we demand justice when innocent blood is spilled?

Have you ever wondered why our hearts are splintered by human suffering in ways that do not match the grief of any other kind of loss? Have you considered why our hearts are moved by human goodness in ways that do not match our joy from any other experience?

We react this way because deep inside every one of us is a sense that humanity matters. As a Christian, I would argue that this idea of human dignity originates in the Christian story. The historian Timothy Shah says that, "apart from the Christian Scriptures, classical civilization lacked the concept of human dignity" (and a cursory read of Roman society makes his point unarguable[2]). Granted, there are traces of this concept in other religions such as Islam and Judaism. There are glimpses of human dignity to be found in the philosophers such as Kant or Locke. But those traces are only filled out in full by the Christian gospel, and those glimpses found in the philosophers or other religions are mere signposts of Christianity's exalted view of humanity.

Even in our secular age, we are still building on the foundations found in the Bible; as one scholar says, attempts to define or explain human dignity are explaining "in non-religious terms a persuasive concept that had long before come to light through Biblical revelation."[3]

That may sound strange, given that human rights seem to be more defined, defended, and talked about today than in any other era of human history. We live in the age of the United Nations, formed 75 years ago in the aftermath of a bloody half-century of war, genocide, and totalitarianism. This body gathered the world's leading thinkers and ethicists to create what became the Universal Declaration on Human Rights, which offers, "recognition of the inherent dignity ... of all members of the human family." Though the UN has a mixed record of consistency on human rights, this document has since been used as a basis to fight genocide and other injustices, to topple corrupt governments and form new ones, and to prosecute war criminals.

---

2 Timothy Shah and Allan D. Hertzke, *Christianity and Freedom: Volume 1, Historical Perspectives (Law and Christianity)* (Cambridge University Press, 2017), page 127.
3 John F. Kilner, *Dignity and Destiny: Humanity in the Image of God* (Eerdmans, 2015), page 7.

WHY DIGNITY?

All of this is good. And yet there is something profoundly interesting and quite disturbing about the way this statement was drafted. This beautiful declaration of human dignity is built on... nothing at all. The ethicist Gilbert Meilaender writes, in his book *Neither Beast Nor God* (emphasis added):

> *"While these philosophers were able to agree on many particular claims, they were perhaps, unsurprisingly,* **unable to agree on 'why' these claims were true**—*unable, that is, to develop any shared vision of human nature or the human person on which such claims could be based."*

These thinkers—the most credentialed ethicists in the world—could articulate that human dignity matters, but could not articulate why. Meilaender says:

> *"I doubt that there is any way to derive a commitment to equal respect for every human being from the ordinary distinctions in merit and excellence that we all use in some spheres of life; it is grounded rather, not in our relation to each other, but in our relation to God."* [4]

In other words, there is no basis for human dignity without a connection to God. Without taking account of the divine, we are left with a view of a human's dignity based on that individual's merit or excellence, based on some societally-agreed or government-imposed yardstick; and if the last century teaches us anything, it is that this shifting metric is dangerous.

This is why the philosopher Oliver O'Donovan says that any idea of human dignity "is, and only can be, a theological

---

4 *Neither Beast Nor God: The Dignity of the Human Person* (Encounter Books, 2009), pages 90, 95.

assertion." [5] Of course this doesn't mean that only Christians have recognized human dignity; nor does this mean Christians have always understand and practiced human dignity well in the cultures in which they were situated (more on that in the next chapter). It certainly does not mean that in our day Christians are always and everywhere treating others with greater dignity than those who reject the gospel. But it remains the case that the basis for the human dignity that is promoted in statements such as the UN declaration is borrowed from the Christian story.

The Bible's robust view of humanity is one of the best gifts Christianity gives to the world.

WHAT HUMAN MEANS

Genesis, the book of beginnings, contains in its first chapter a profound definition of what it means be human. Moses, the human author of the opening book of the Bible, contrasts the origins of animal and plant life with the origins of humanity. He uses exalted language to describe God's crafting of human existence. The rest of creation is spoken into existence by the word of God, but human life is sculpted by the hands of God from the dust of the ground. Into humans was breathed the breath of life (2 v 7). And, most importantly, humans are, as Moses mentions twice in the creation account, created "in the image of God":

> Then God said, "Let us make man in our image, after our likeness. And let them have dominion over the fish of the sea and over the birds of the heavens and over the livestock and over all the earth and over every creeping thing that creeps on the earth." So God created man in his own image, in the image of God he created him; male and female he created them. GENESIS 1 V 26-27

---

5 Quoted in Meilaender, *Neither Beast Nor God*, page 90.

There is much beauty and mystery here. To begin with, we are being shown that the creation of humans was a divine event in the councils of the triune God. "Let us make man in our image" implies a discussion among the Godhead: Father, Son, and Spirit. Nowhere else in God's creative acts is this kind of deliberation suggested. No other part of creation, from stars to starfish, is described with such specific and exalted language.

So what exactly does it mean to be created "in the image of God?" It means both that we are not God and also that we are not animals or angels. To acknowledge the fact that we are made in his image means both embracing humility and enjoying dignity.

Our dignity flows from and is rooted in the truth that we are like God. You are more than simply the sum of your parts. You are not merely a highly evolved mammal. You are not just a collection of atoms. You are not just what others see or the combination of others' verdicts on you. You are made in the image of God: crowned, the psalmist writes, "with glory and honor" (Psalm 8 v 5).

Our humility grows in the soil of the truth that we are not God. You are not the center of your own universe, the master of your own fate. You are not the arbiter of right and wrong. You cannot find sufficient reason for your existence or fulfillment in your existence from within.

Part of being made in his image means that God has bestowed on us certain God-like characteristics, such as the ability to reason, to think, to create, to love, to mourn. These are abilities that make us distinct from even the highest forms of the rest of creation. We must be careful, however (as we will see in the next chapter), not to reduce what it means to bear the image of God to mere function. If we limit human dignity simply to these uniquely human traits, it has a disastrous impact on the way we see those whose cognitive, God-like abilities have been diminished in one way or another and for one reason or another. The view that worth is based exclusively on certain virtues or gifts or contributions to society makes dignity and worth fleeting and uncertain, and opens the door to deciding that certain groups have less God-given dignity than others.

It is dangerous to reduce the ground of human dignity to what we do or what we offer, rather than who we are. Just as God is known by his actions but not defined by his actions, so are those made in his image. You were valuable before you did anything. I would still be valuable even if I were rendered unable to do anything.

WITH PRIVILEGE COMES RESPONSIBILITY

Being made in God's image also gives us certain God-given responsibilities. We are not God; we are, instead, under God. In *Created in God's Image*, Anthony Hoekema writes:

> *"When one sees a human being, one ought to see in him or her a certain reflection of God ... In the creation of man, God revealed himself in a unique way, by making someone who was a kind of mirror image of himself. No higher honor could have been given to man than the privilege of being an image of God, who made him."* [6]

To the extent that we mirror God, we also represent God in the world. In the ancient world, it was common for kings to construct images of themselves and place them throughout their kingdoms in order to be represented when they couldn't be present. These images spoke silently, saying, *The king is still ruling. Don't forget this place has a ruler.* In some ways, our image-rich culture understands this well. We put pics or avatars or headshots of ourselves

---

6 *Created in God's Image* (Eerdmans, 1994), page 67.

on our social-media accounts. An image of me on my Twitter profile stands as a representation of me.

But this only scratches the surface of what God intended when he created humans to be his imagers in the world. We are called to be his representatives in his creation. We were created to glorify God by loving what he loves, acting as he acts, living as he lives (Ephesians 2 v 10). In creating humanity, God gave us a mandate to rule and to create, to love and to lead:

> *Be fruitful and multiply and fill the earth and subdue it,*
> *and have dominion over the fish of the sea and over the*
> *birds of the heavens and over every living thing that moves*
> *on the earth.* GENESIS 1 V 28

One way to understand this is to think of human dignity "structurally" and "directionally":[7]

- *Structurally*, we have dignity and worth, regardless of our usefulness or our mistakes, because we were created after God's image.
- *Directionally*, we were created to image God to everyone and everything around us, as a response to our unique place in his creation.

We don't simply enjoy being made in God's image. We are to live it out in how we relate to the rest of his creation. We are not gods, and this world is not here to serve and worship us; we are mere imagers or image-bearers of the triune God. This involves responsibility: most specifically to represent God in his world, by caring for his creation and his creatures, and filling the earth with his glory.

---

7 I have to credit my friend Bruce Ashford, Provost at Southeastern Baptist Theological Seminary, for this language of "structural and directional," in conversations and edits for this chapter. I'd recommend reading and interacting with Bruce's work. He's one of the sharpest thinkers in the evangelical world.

UNDERSTANDING IS NOT THE SAME AS LIVING

At a basic level, Christians have always understood this. But it's possible that we have not fully wrestled with its profound implications for how we see ourselves, how we see God, and how we live in the world. Every generation of the church has struggled to reckon with the full implications of this theology. Today is no different. While most of us know humans are created in the image of God, we often fail to recognize the image of God in others. Or we recognize it in some groups of people but fail to recognize it in others.

In a technologically-advanced world where we are increasingly made aware of assaults on human dignity through racism, war, violence, and disease, we are often confused at how to react or about what a Christian response looks like. This is why it is urgent for followers of Jesus to see that a conscious recovery of the idea of human dignity is what enables us to engage a complex world in how we think, what we say, and how we act.

A passive or deficient understanding of human dignity is harmful both for our sense of self-worth and for our ability to live out the Great Commission—to go into the world and share the good news of Christ's death and resurrection (Matthew 28 v 18-20); and the Great Commandment—to love God fully and to love our neighbor as ourselves (Mark 12 v 29-31). If we don't keep front and center the dignity, humility, and responsibility that is grounded in being made in God's image, we won't see sin as serious and tragic, and we won't see the urgency of sharing the gospel declaration that humans can be restored to their Creator and to their purpose. And if we don't keep front and center that great truth that every person is a person made in God's image, then we prove to be callously indifferent (in our actions if not in our emotions) to the needs of our neighbors.

The world needs the church to recover a Christian vision for human dignity.

THE IMAGE OF GOD

It is important for us to understand the Bible's specific language here. The biblical writers were careful, when referring to humans, to insert a preposition. Humans are created after or in the image of God. Only one human being is ever described as being the perfect image of God: Jesus Christ. In 2 Corinthians 4 v 4 and Colossians 1 v 15, the apostle Paul reminds his readers that it is Christ who is the image of God. The writer of Hebrews says Jesus is "the exact imprint of [God's] nature" (Hebrews 1 v 3).

You and I are made *in* the image of God. Jesus Christ, fully God and fully man, *is* the image of God.

Jesus Christ is the fullest embodiment of the image of God: the only human who fully embodies what it means to fulfill our mandate as image-bearers, to live out that dignity and humility and responsibility. And he is the Creator God. In him we see the Creator become creature—that is the wonder of the first Christmas. The life, death, and resurrection of Jesus not only gives us definitions for what it means to be human, but holds out to us the offer of being remade as the humans we should be, and have failed to be.

This is what makes the Christian vision of human dignity so unique. It does not only tell us what we ought to be; it gives us all we need to be remade into what we ought to be. The Bible reveals that it was God's eternal purpose to create mankind to reflect the image of Christ: "Those whom he foreknew he also predestined to be conformed to the image of his Son" (Romans 8 v 29); and that it is through Christ's death and resurrection that God restores us to our image-bearing glory and purposes: "If anyone is in Christ, he is a new creation [for] God ... through Christ, reconciled us to himself" (2 Corinthians 5 v 17, 18).

The theologian Thomas Schreiner says it best: Jesus is, "the agenda of creation and the goal of creation."[8]

THE CHURCH AT ITS BEST

Image-bearing, image-based human dignity is not a new concept. At its best, the church has allowed this belief to shape the way it has acted on behalf of vulnerable people. We could go so far as to say that the church has most fulfilled its task when this belief has been most celebrated. The theology of human dignity has informed Christian witness, in some form or another, for 2,000 years. Toward the end of the first century, the Christian leader Clement of Rome told believers:

> *"You should do good to and pay honor and reverence to man, who is made in the image of God ... minister food to the hungry, drink to the thirsty, clothing to the naked, hospitality to the stranger, and necessary things to the prisoner; and that is what will be regarded as truly bestowed upon God."*[9]

Lactantius, in his 3rd-century *Divine Institutes*, argued for the uniqueness of mankind above the rest of creation. Gregory of Nyssa in the 4th century wrote of man that he is "in his being in the image of the nature of the creator." In the 5th century Augustine, both in his *Confessions* and in his commentary on Genesis, marveled at the greatness of humanity—a greatness he ascribed to God's creative acts. You can find a similar thread throughout church history,

---

8 *Paul, Apostle of God's Glory in Christ: A Pauline Theology* (IVP Academic, 2006), page 156..

9 *The Recognitions of Clement*, edited and revised Douglas F. Hatten (Douglas F. Hatten, 2007), page 185

from the fathers of the first six centuries of the church to the medieval scholastics, through the Reformation in the 1500s and 1600s, and on into the present.

Yet at the same time, we must admit that, when it comes to treating all people as being made in God image, the behavior of some Christians and churches has been far from perfect. Tragically, there have been Christians who have used the Bible to either justify or ignore racism, slavery, and genocide. At times the church has had to learn from those outside the church what it means to treat particular groups in a way that is consistent with what biblical believers profess to believe. I would argue that these dignity-diminishing views and actions have either been a deviation from, or a willing ignorance of, God's view of humanity as revealed in his word. And it is always a recovery of Christian theology that has moved Christians to repent of sinful ideologies and work for justice in the world.

Today the challenges to human dignity are as serious as those that have faced any generation. War, poverty, racism, abortion, violence, slavery, and other injustices prey upon the dignity of humans everywhere. This is why a recovery of a robust Christian vision of human dignity is vital if we are to represent God as his imagers in this world. If our generation would leave a legacy that our spiritual grandchildren will be proud of, and that the world may one day be thankful for, we must learn what it means to really live out what we say we believe: that every person we meet, interact with, or hear of carries inalienable dignity, made as they are in God's image.

Without this, we will have incomplete tools for loving our neighbor and carrying out the mission of God. And we will succumb to the temptations of the church in every generation to ignore or even justify injustice or prioritize the dignity of one group of people at the expense or in ignorance of another.

Human dignity is not just a political buzzword or theological concept. A right view of human dignity is essential to a right view of ourselves, of our God, and of the world that he made and in which we live. It is—or should be—at the heart of what we think and how we act as the people of God. It is—or should be—the foundation of our unyielding determination to say, and to live out, the truth that a person's a person—no matter how small.

2. LOSING OUR HUMANITY

"If man is not made in the image of God, nothing then stands in the way of inhumanity."

FRANCIS SCHAEFFER

At first, the grainy, sped-up, black-and white footage of men, women, and children being lined up and shot, their bodies kicked into open graves, looks like something from a silent film.

But these are images from a real event.

Later, as I walk through the cool, narrow corridors of Yad Vashem, the Holocaust museum in Jerusalem, listening to the narrator walk me through history, looking at the brutal instruments of death, and running my hands along the artifacts collected from the people that had been killed, everything feels somehow strange and otherworldly as the horrendous truth closes in on me that the horrors depicted and described in this place did not happen inside a movie, but happened in this world and happened to real people.

Some of them are in my family tree.

My mother is Jewish. My great-grandparents fled Poland and Russia at the turn of the 19th century in search of a better life. But if they hadn't—and their emigration was perilous and uncertain—perhaps I would never have stood viewing footage of human atrocities. Perhaps—probably—it would have been my grandparents falling into those open graves.

There in that museum, I wept as I saw piles of shoes, glasses, children's toys. People, people, people with hopes and dreams, people ruthlessly hunted, captured, and killed. In a large, round room that looked like a planetarium, stars on the ceiling represented children. 1.5 million of them. In each star, I imagined the face of one of my children, vulnerable and innocent, marked for death.

#NEVERAGAIN?

The question most often asked in the narrowing corridors of Yad Vashem is, "How could people let this happen?" And there is an interesting assumption that lies behind that question—an assumption that is unsettling to unearth. It is this: we doubt our own ability to either perpetrate or tolerate such evil. When we ask, "How could people let this happen?" we are saying that we are convinced that such a thing would be impossible in our society in our day. We have convinced ourselves that the progress of history means today's world—or at least, the part of today's world in which we live—is no longer capable of witnessing, allowing, or perpetrating heinous acts. We have persuaded ourselves that saying, or tweeting, #Neveragain can be more than an aspiration.

History suggests differently. The Nazi regime didn't come to power in a developing nation under the spell of pagan ideologies. Hitler rose to power in 20th-century Germany, in a civilized and predominately outwardly Christian country.

And still today, in nature though perhaps not in degree, we see these things happening. Literally today, as I write this, I've read about a bombing at an Ariana Grande concert attended mainly by young girls and their parents in Manchester, England. I've read about a bus full of Coptic Christians in Egypt slaughtered by a radical Islamist gunman. I've read about a resort in the Philippines where lie 23 dead bodies, the result of a random shooting spree by a disgruntled tourist.

This is just one week. Soon new atrocities will cross my timeline. And these are merely the news stories of which I'm aware, if I'm paying attention at that particular moment. As you read this, civil wars, man-made famines, and ethnic cleansing are sending humans to early graves. Life, even in the safe corridors of the West, is becoming increasingly cheap and disposable, and is feeling increasingly uncertain and insecure.

Why is there such a deep chasm between the beautiful theology of Genesis 1 and the violent reality of our world? What has happened that causes God's image-bearers to invent more and more sophisticated and more efficient ways to turn against each other?

The Bible has a rather blunt answer—an answer that falls hard on post-modern ears and has, I fear, become a kind of mindless incantation for some Christians.

This chapter is not easy for some to read. For others, it will sound very familiar—perhaps too familiar. But we skip this at our peril. Without it, we cannot look reality in the face and at the same time live with hope; and we cannot make a real, lasting difference in the real world.

We need to talk about sin.

WHY DO HUMANS DEVALUE HUMANITY?

Something has happened. Even our most compelling stories, told in bestselling novels and big-budget movies and downloaded in music from iTunes, echo what our hearts tell us—that the world should be good, but is now maddeningly broken. Hardwired into our psyche is an intuition that things are both beautiful, and should be—and that they are broken, and should not be. The Genesis account is, I think, the only one that gives sufficient explanation both for what we see in this world and in our own lives and hearts.

The first humans, Adam and Eve, created in innocence and beauty by a loving God, chose to follow the way of the serpent instead of the way of their Creator. Genesis 3 recounts how, rather than enjoy intimacy with their Creator, the first humans chose to heed the seductive whispers of Satan that, if they ate the one fruit God had ruled off-limits, "You will be like God" (Genesis 3 v 5). They "worshiped and served the creature rather than the Creator" (Romans 1 v 25)—and they plunged the human race into sin and corruption and death. Those made to be like God decided that they would try to be God. Those created to know God struck out for a world where they hoped there would be no God.

We tend to think of sin as a kind of benign mistake. Comedians joke about their sins. Christians smile benevolently and excuse themselves and each other for their sins (often while bemoaning those of other people outside their church or social bracket). Chocolate is marketed as "sinfully delicious." Well, chocolate is just chocolate. But real sin always promises to taste delicious and it always lies. And it didn't take long for Adam's eating from the forbidden tree to bear rotten fruit. It embedded a deep and pervasive corruption in human hearts, a corruption that "brings forth death" (James 1 v 15). Sin is no plaything. Sin is devastating.

Sin is what dehumanizes us. To be fully human is to enjoy bearing God's image, in the joy of relationship with him. But sinful humanity flees the relationship for which they were made—Adam and Eve used the garden God had given them to seek to hide from him (Genesis 3 v 8). And sin causes us to dehumanize others. Happy in God, to be fully human is to enjoy trusting, other-centered relationship with other image-bearing humans. But sinful humans seek to distance themselves in mistrust, and to use others in selfishness—Adam and Eve covered themselves up in each others' presence, and Adam then sought to blame Eve for his own sin in order to excuse himself before God (v 7, 12).

A rejection of the image-giver always results in injustice against image-bearers. Death flows downhill from sin. Adam and Eve's son Cain, riven by envy and driven by anger, struck out against his brother Abel, and committed the first act of bloodshed. Listen to the words of rebuke that God issues toward Cain in response to his act of murder:

> *And the* LORD *said, "What have you done? The voice of your brother's blood is crying to me from the ground. And now you are cursed from the ground, which has opened its mouth to receive your brother's blood from your hand."*
>
> GENESIS 4 V 10-11

Cain slew Abel when nobody was looking. He hid the body. He had, it seemed, pulled off the perfect crime. And yet… the Creator who formed and fashioned Abel in his image says to Cain that this innocent blood cries up to him from the ground.

Violence against a fellow human is a direct assault on the authority of God. To strike at an image-bearer to is to strike at the One in whose image that person was created. The kings of God's Old Testament people who rightly worshiped God always knocked down the graven images of other gods. To strike down an icon of a god was to say that that god was no longer the object of worship. Abel was made in the image of God; and so is every other human.

The ground has been soaking up such blood for thousands of years now. It still is. Since Eden, the human race has been repeating this cycle of violence and death. Holocausts happen because humans, corrupted by sin, turn on one another. The most terrible and the most everyday dehumanizing of one human by another or one group by another is not a strange throwback to a more medieval era. It is the rotten fruit of the human race's deal with the devil.

THE GOOD NEWS OF TOTAL DEPRAVITY

The biblical concept of "original sin" states simply that humans, as a result of Adam's choice, are fundamentally corrupted by sin (Romans 5 v 12). Among the physical and personality characteristics parents pass onto their children, two things are always handed down: sin and death. As King David put it, "I was sinful at birth, sinful from the time my mother conceived me" (Psalm 51 v 5, NIV). There are degrees of goodness in each of us and shades of corruption in each of us. Those who don't follow God are capable, by their God-given design, of being loving and doing good. But all of us do have a natural inclination to turn inward and worship ourselves and turn outward in violence against our fellow image-bearer.

Flowing from that is the doctrine of "total depravity"—the truth that though humans are not as bad as they could be, no human act is as good as it could and should be, because everything is tainted by our natural rejection of God as God.

It's not chic, in polite society, to speak of humans as depraved. Most modern philosophy offers some version of the idea that humans are basically good creatures and only act violently as a result of a disadvantaged environment. It is, of course, true that a variety of systemic and social factors do play a role in squeezing people into situations where violence seems to be the only way to survive, but it doesn't offer a full and satisfying explanation.

It doesn't explain why young men and women from affluent homes in affluent Western democracies join ISIS.

It doesn't explain how a monster can arise from a civilized nation like Germany in a century marked by the greatest technological advancement in human history.

It doesn't explain why racism and the Jim Crow laws that enforced racial segregation could germinate in the south of the United States—the region of the country most marked by religious faith.

It doesn't explain why all our efforts at securing and maintaining love and harmony so often, sooner or later, prove only to go skin-deep.

It doesn't explain why, even at its best, religion and virtue may ameliorate but never can eradicate sin.

And ironically, a view of wrongdoing that reduces it to the product of a person's upbringing and environment is in itself deeply dehumanizing. It ends up claiming that we have no real choice, no real freedom. If my decisions can be explained sufficiently by factors outside of myself, I am a mere unwitting automaton, with no agency. The doctrine of sin says that I am responsible. I am free to choose. I am human. The tragedy is that, so often, I choose wrong.

Why? Because "the heart is deceitful above all things, and desperately sick; who can understand it?" (Jeremiah 17 v 9).

THE CROSS IS GREATER

You might be reading this and thinking, *Wow, Dan, this is pretty hopeless.* And you would be right—if the story the Bible tells ended in Genesis chapter four. The world is hopeless if all we have is the endless parade of sin and death we see scroll across our social-media timelines and flash before us on our TV screens. The world is hopeless if all we have is the deep corruption we see in the communities and cities in which we live. The world is hopeless if all we have are the dark passions that war against us in our souls.

In the narrative of Cain and Abel, Cain replies to God, "My punishment is greater than I can bear." And so it is. But it is only when sinful humans cry out in echo of sinful Cain that the great truth of the New Testament comes into glorious focus:

> *Christ ... suffered for you ... He himself bore our sins in his body on the tree ... By his wounds you have been healed.*
>
> 1 PETER 2 V 21, 24

The idea of original sin seems harsh, and it violates our modern sensibilities—but it is actually the gateway to the best news you could possibly hear. The gospel story tells us that we can face reality without needing to excuse ourselves. What Cain could not bear and what I cannot bear and what you cannot bear—guilt and the shame it brings now and the judgment it earns beyond death—Christ bore. The gospel tells us both that the crisis is worse than modern man is willing to confront and that the cross of Christ is greater than modern man can ever realize. Not only does Christ offer us forgiveness through his cross but he also offers us his Spirit, "that we might die to sin and live to righteousness" (v 24)—that we might, with new hearts, turn toward our Creator in worship and toward our fellow man in love as we await his return to make all things new. As the hymn-writer Charles Wesley put it, "Second Adam from above, reinstate us in thy love."

DEHUMANIZATION AND THE CHURCH

But things are not new yet. Yad Vashem will continue to stand as one of many monuments to the worst effects of our bent toward dehumanizing others. What has haunted me since my visit is the gigantic wall displaying a timeline of art during the Third Reich. I cannot shake the memory of the way in which anti-Semitic artists portrayed Jewish people. It was a slow, systematic dehumanizing of a people group. People were portrayed as villains. Then, villains were portrayed as unenlightened. Then, the unenlightened were portrayed as animals. And so Jews became rats. People made in God's image—disabled people, gay and lesbian people, gypsies, the list goes on and on—became *untermenschen* (subhuman). People become problems and a desire for compassion is replaced by a search for solution.

And so it was that a failure to see native Americans as fully human or possessing the full image of God led to many in the colonial period to excuse atrocities against them. Oliver Wendell Holmes Sr., a Harvard lawyer and father of the future United States Supreme Court Justice, celebrated the demise of native Americans by declaring that "the red-crayon sketch is rubbed out and the canvas is ready for a picture of manhood a little more like God's image."[10]

This same bent toward dehumanizing people enabled Americans to participate in the trafficking, selling, and ownership of black slaves during much of the history of the US, and even to enshrine this sinful concept of sub-humanity in law with a compromise which saw African Americans counted as three-fifths of a human. Nearly a century later, as Martin Luther King Jr. marched for the civil rights of minorities, he famously declared, "I am a man"—because he recognized that the question of humanity lay at the heart of the issue of civil rights and indeed of racism itself.

Sadly, at times Christians have been more swayed by their culture than their Scriptures. It was a Christian publishing

---

10 Thomas F. Gossett, *Race: The History of an Idea in America* (Oxford University Press, 1997), page 243.

house that in 1901 released a book by the influential Unitarian leader Charles Carroll, *The Negro a Beast or In the Image of God,* which made the case that white people were made in the image of God while black people were patterned after "some other model." It was pastors of evangelical churches who echoed those ideas in their pulpits during the height of the civil rights movement in the 1960's, many white evangelical pastors in the South.

It was theologians such as Emil Brunner who argued that the image of God was diminished in those who don't possess rational capacities, such as some of those who are mentally disabled.[11] Even some of our favorite and important theologians, like Martin Luther and Thomas Aquinas, saw diminished mental capacity as evidence for diminished dignity due to the fall.[12]

Today, we might be past the era when African-Americans are sold as slaves in America and Great Britain—but we are clearly not beyond the ugly scourge of racism. We might think we are beyond the capacity for the evil of the Third Reich—but don't doubt that we can still dehumanize entire classes of people. Just listen to the rhetoric often used to describe undesired vulnerable people groups. It is not uncommon to hear immigrants described as "riff-raff," "trash," or "illegals"—never "people"—or unborn humans described as clumps of tissue, collections of cells, or fetuses—never "people." We see it in the way we refer to minority groups with the dehumanizing article "the." When we don't see people there, we start to free our consciences to accept or commit violence and death against our fellow humans.

After all, our views have already been warped by the application of Darwinism to relationships within our own

11 Brunner, *Natural Theology* (Wipf and Stock, 2002), page 57.
12 See, for instance, Aquinas, *Summa Theologica*, page 93.

race. Again, a thorough-going adherence to the principle of "survival of the fittest" within humanity reached a nadir (or one of them) in the Nazi extermination camps. But in a thousand ways, in a thousand interactions and judgments, we live out, without even noticing, this idea that the victory belongs to the swiftest, and the devil can take the hindmost. Think, for instance, about our commitment to meritocracy. It is not a big step to ascribe greater dignity to those who are worth more. This is not the book to debate the role (or lack of it) of evolution in the way God created his world. It is the place to point out that applying the model to our human relationships is always catastrophic, as the German theologian Jürgen Moltmann warned:

> "Evolution always means selection. Many living things are sacrificed in order that 'the fittest,'—which means the most effective and the most adaptable—may survive. In this way higher and increasingly complex life systems, which can react to changed environments, undoubtedly develop. But in the same process milliards of living things fall by the wayside and disappear into evolution's rubbish bin. Evolution is not merely a constructive affair on nature's part. It is a cruel one too. It is a kind of biological execution of the Last Judgment on the weak, the sick and the 'unfit.'" [13]

Perhaps the greatest danger is that we assume that our age, and our Christian tribe, has avoided the mistakes of our nation's ancestors and of our spiritual forefathers, and always treats humans with dignity. If you cannot believe that Christians kept quiet during the Holocaust, undermined the dignity of people who are disabled, and actively promoted the idea that people were more or less worthy

---

13 Richard Bauckham, *Theology of Jürgen Moltmann* (Bloomsbury Publishing, 1995), page 19.

based on the color of their skin, ask yourself, "What might people in 200 years struggle to believe that I thought, or remained quiet about, or actively supported?"

SIN-STAINED, BUT STILL IMAGE-BEARERS

Scripture stands against this idea of diminished dignity in any human. Sin corrupts all of us—but our status as image-bearers always remains intact.

In Genesis 9 v 6, we find God giving these instructions to Noah as he and his family rebuild the human race after the flood (and therefore, crucially, after the fall):

> *Whoever sheds the blood of man, by man shall his blood be shed, for God made man in his own image.*

Notice the logic: because humans are made by God in his image, every human life—every drop of human blood—matters. In a fallen world, the stamp of the image of God has not been diminished. And that matters when it comes not only to extreme assaults on that image such as murder, but in more insidious attacks on it such as our speech:

> *With [our tongue] we bless our Lord and Father, and with it we curse people who are made in the likeness of God.*
>
> JAMES 3 V 9

Fallen we may all be, failures we all are, but dignity we still own. There is no situation in which we may ignore the fact that every person is an image-bearing person. No disease or disability lessens a person's possession of the image of God. We can never reduce someone's humanity to their utility—to their usefulness to society. There are no exemptions, no asterisks, placed against the truth that man is made in God's image and that this is where we derive our value.

I recently listened to a radio interview with a political candidate running for office in the US. My ears pricked up because the interviewer asked him about his views on abortion. "George," the candidate said,

"I used to be pro-choice, but a few years ago a friend of mine had a child. The pregnancy was inconvenient and they had considered terminating, but they chose, at the last minute, to keep the baby. I've seen how this child has grown up to be such a bright and talented young man. I can't imagine killing such a gifted child. So I'm pro-life. We are killing the next generation."

Now, I am pro-life. I agree that the person in the womb is a person (see chapter five). But I think this pro-life candidate's thinking is deeply dangerous, and that matters even though he has perhaps landed in the same place as me on this contentious issue. Here's why. He said he had changed his mind because that child had grown up to be "such a bright and talented young man." But what if he had grown up to be very, very average? What if he had grown up disabled, with reduced mental abilities? He changed his mind because we shouldn't kill potentially gifted future children. But what about the ordinary future children? The disabled future children? The children of the future who have special needs? What about them?

Our view of human dignity must be based on every person being made in God's image, and not on clever arguments based on utility. In fact, as theologian Walter Pannenberg says, if anything it is the seemingly weaker among us that enable us to see the wonder and the security that come from knowing we are all made in the image of God:

"In a special way, because they have nothing else that commands respect, the faces of the suffering and humbled and deprived are ennobled by the reflection of this dignity that

none of us has by merit, that none of us can receive from others, and that no one can take from us." [14]

Everyone—no matter who they are, what they offer, or what they've done—has value and dignity because they were created by God. Nothing anyone can do or lacks can change that. Everyone is an image-bearer. And everyone is a sinner; which means that every image-bearer finds it natural to think that everyone else (or even themselves) is not an image-bearer. And therein lies the seeds of every murder, every war, every act of self-harm.

A LIST THAT SHOULD BE LONGER

As visitors leave Yad Vashem, the narrow and dark corridors open up to bright sunlight over a beautiful green space—the Garden of the Righteous Among the Nations. This garden is dedicated to Gentiles who risked everything to protect and save Jews. The names are part of a roster of those who saw the inhumanity of the Holocaust—and who fought back, who quietly risked everything to protect the lives, the dignity, of those who were being treated as *untermenschen.*

The size of the list both broke and challenged my heart. It should be longer.

And I wonder, had I been a German Christian, living under the rule of the Third Reich, would I have possessed the unyielding conviction to resist the pressure to conform, to see the Jews as less than human? Would I have had the courage to step forward and affirm in my actions the dignity of those being sent off to their deaths, even at a high cost to my own privilege? The sobering reality is that those who chose to oppose injustice in that generation were the exception rather than the rule. May it be

---

14 Pannenberg, *Systematic Theology,* page 173.

us—may it be you—who live as the exception to the rule in our generation, whenever and wherever and however our fellows humans are treated as though they have diminished dignity.

May it be us—may it be you—who are remembered as those who resisted cultural pressures, resisted temptation to put ourselves above others, and who worked for justice for those whose voices had been silenced. May it be us—may it be you—who work to safeguard and celebrate the dignity of every person, even—especially—those who are all too easily forgotten and diminished by our culture.

3. DIGNITY REDISCOVERED

"It's a strange, poor population God has in his kingdom."
GRAHAM GREENE

"I didn't depose a king to become a king," George Washington supposedly said of the idea of him becoming monarch of the newly formed United States. The US was formed through rejection of monarchy (though, given our fascination with the British royal family, you would not necessarily know it). And in Europe, absolute monarchies are a thing of the past—the castles and ceremonies may remain, but the power they were once the public projection of has long since waned.

We therefore find ourselves in a strange period of human history. We are simply not accustomed to kingdoms and empires in the way that they have been understood for most of world history. In an era of democracy and populism, few of us have an understanding of the role of kings and the scope of kingdoms. We think of them as quaint relics of another era or the kind of dangerous concentration of power whose yoke the people would be wise to throw off.

And yet there is a lot of language in the Bible about the kingdom of God. Jesus often used this language. In fact, it is impossible to talk about human dignity without talking about the kingdom of God: what it is and what it requires of those whom God is calling to be citizens of that kingdom.

WHAT'S SO GREAT ABOUT THE KINGDOM?

When we think of a king and a kingdom, we typically think of "pomp and circumstance" and castles. But at its most basic level, a kingdom is simply an area, or a people, under the dominion of a king. And so the kingdom is only ever as good or bad, as glorious or flawed, as its king (Proverbs 29 v 2).

I'm not a historian, but I love reading biographies and listening to lectures on history. In my amateur studies, I've noticed the power of leadership. Countries often come to reflect the character of those who lead them. The qualities of a nation's most revered leaders are the qualities that the nation protects and promotes.

This is what the Scripture, I believe, is getting at when it describes the kingdom of God. What is the kingdom of God like? It is like the character of God. That is why the psalmist says to God:

> *You are good and do good; teach me your statutes.*
>
> PSALM 119 V 68

He is saying, in effect, *God, you are completely good and you always do good; therefore I trust you and ask you to teach me the laws that will show me how to do good.*

Imagine, for a moment, what the world would look like if it functioned as it should. If people treated each other with love and dignity and grace... If promises were kept and the vulnerable were protected... If natural disasters didn't kill and destroy... If animals and plant life lived in perfect harmony... If disease and decay and violence were no longer a part of our existence. I imagine that the longing for that kind of better world pulsates in your heart.

And that longing is, whether we think of it this way or not, a longing for the kingdom of God.

Throughout the Old Testament the prophets talked of a time of restoration and harmony and beauty:

> *The wolf shall dwell with the lamb,*
> *and the leopard shall lie down with the young goat,*
> *and the calf and the lion and the fattened calf together;*
> *and a little child shall lead them.*
> *The cow and the bear shall graze;*
> *their young shall lie down together;*
> *and the lion shall eat straw like the ox.*
> *The nursing child shall play over the hole of the cobra,*
> *and the weaned child shall put his hand on the adder's den.*
> *They shall not hurt or destroy*
> *in all my holy mountain;*
> *for the earth shall be full of the knowledge of the LORD*
> *as the waters cover the sea.* ISAIAH 11 V 6-9

This vision of a coming kingdom of peace pulsates throughout the Old Testament in stark contrast to the human kingdoms of the world, which, even at their best, cannot bring ultimate peace and flourishing. Old Testament Israel provided glimpses of this coming kingdom of God, when they had a good king. But even the best rulers were mere shadows of the coming King who would ultimately emerge from the family of David, Israel's greatest earthly king (2 Samuel 7 v 12-17; Psalm 89 v 28-37).

But Israel's kings were trampled and finally overthrown by invasion and exile. Still the prophets spoke of the future, full kingdom of God. But then, after the last prophet spoke, there were four hundred years of silence from God. No more prophets. No more kings. No more revelations.

And then, God spoke through unconventional but history-changing means. He spoke by coming—by coming, as the prophets foretold, as a baby, born to an otherwise obscure virgin girl in a small town in Palestine, a Roman province. Heavenly messengers were sent to announce that this was the one who came from David's family and who would rule on David's throne forever (Luke 1 v 30-33)— that here was good news of great joy:

> *Unto you is born this day in the city of David a Savior,*
> *who is Christ the Lord. And this will be a sign for you:*
> *you will find a baby wrapped in swaddling cloths and lying*
> *in a manger.*   LUKE 2 V 11-12

This, the angels declare to Mary and to the shepherds, is the long-awaited King. A quite unconventional king who landed not in Herod's pristine palace or Caesar's opulent palace, but in an animal shelter in Bethlehem, the hamlet that the prophet Micah, centuries before, had named as the place where he would be born:

> *But you, O Bethlehem Ephrathah, who are too little to be*
> *among the clans of Judah, from you shall come forth for me*
> *one who is to be ruler in Israel, whose coming forth is from*
> *of old, from ancient days.*   MICAH 5 V 2

Here is the announcement that the King is here, and therefore the kingdom has begun. The new kingdom, then, is not embodied in a country or an earthly human government but in a person: Jesus Christ. Listen to Jesus' own words, as he began his adult ministry:

> *Now after John was arrested, Jesus came into Galilee,*
> *proclaiming the gospel of God, and saying, "The time is*
> *fulfilled, and the kingdom of God is at hand; repent and*
> *believe in the gospel."*   MARK 1 V 14-15

THE KING HAS COME

Let's unpack what Jesus is saying here. First he says the simple phrase, "The time is fulfilled." If you were a first-century Jew, you were being told that the time you had longed for had, after four hundred years of silence, many false messiahs, and a millennium of waiting, finally arrived.

Then Jesus says, 'The kingdom of God is at hand." Jesus is saying that the promised kingdom is now here. This is strange talk by Jesus. First, how could the kingdom of God be present when, every day, God's people woke up to the sound of Roman soldiers on patrol in their promised land, and to the sight of a hideous Roman flag standing menacingly in the grounds of their temple? And second, why is he speaking this way not at that temple in Jerusalem, or in the court of the king, but by a large northern lake far from the centers of power? The point Jesus is making is that the kingdom is present because the King is present. Wherever Jesus is, there is the kingdom of God, for the kingdom can be best defined (to borrow from Graeme Goldsworthy) as "God's people in God's place under the rule and blessing of God's King."[15]

In Jesus, the kingdom of God came near. In his words and actions, we see glimpses of the future, full kingdom. Jesus, as Lord of creation, calms the storms (Mark 4 v 35-41), heals the sick (Matthew 8, etc.), feeds the hungry (Matthew 14; Mark 6; John 6), and raises the dead (Matthew 9 v 18-26; Mark 5 v 21-43; John 11). When the imprisoned John the Baptist sends his disciples to Jesus to check if Jesus is indeed the King promised by the prophets, Jesus points to these acts:

---

15 I highly recommend Graeme Goldsworthy, *Gospel and Kingdom* (Paternoster, 2012), as well as Vaughan Roberts, *God's Big Picture: Tracing the Storyline of the Bible* (IVP UK, 2003).

*Go and tell John what you have seen and heard: the blind
receive their sight, the lame walk, lepers are cleansed, and
the deaf hear, the dead are raised up, the poor have good
news preached to them.* LUKE 7 V 22

Jesus' earthly life previewed what the kingdom will look
like: a place of kindness and diversity, dignity and life. The
least and most ignored and rejected people in society are
recognized, cared for, lifted up, even moved to positions
of power. This is a kingdom of dignity and of humanity,
because its King is one of compassion and humility. There
is a new kingdom, Jesus is announcing, and it replaces the
broken kingdom structures of the old world. And require-
ments for citizenship are simple:

Repent and believe in the gospel. MARK 1 V 15

This is the citizenship ceremony. This is what brings us
into God's new kingdom—repenting of our self-rule and
coming under Jesus' perfect rule, and believing that Jesus
has done everything necessary in his death and resurrection to bring us into his kingdom. Jesus brings us into the
kingdom to make us into citizens who reflect that kingdom by being like its king—people made, and remade, in
his image. It is in a kingdom, in obedience to its King, that
we discover the true nature of humanity and experience it
for ourselves. To live out our image-bearing purposes and
to be most free to be ourselves, we must obey Jesus and
continually repent and believe the gospel.

Of course, despite our citizenship in God's kingdom,
our continuing everyday brokenness reminds us that the
kingdom of God has not come in its fullest form. The
King is now reigning in heaven, awaiting his return in
power and glory. His citizens still live in this world, a
world rebelling against its rightful ruler. Those citizens—

the church—in the here and now live as an outpost of the full and future kingdom of God (Matthew 16 v 19; Luke 12 v 32). Jesus is, in himself, the fulfillment of the kingdom promises of the Old Testament (2 Corinthians 1 v 20) and is creating, in the church, a new kind of people from every nation, tribe, and tongue. Wherever and whenever his people gather, there is the kingdom of God (Matthew 18 v 20).

A CHURCH THAT SMELLS LIKE DIGNITY

This kingdom reality has widespread implications for the church's mission. It is a two-fold mission: one of communication and of illumination.

First, we have been tasked with going into the world and preaching the good news that the kingdom of God is both here and is coming. We announced to image-bearers who have rejected their Maker that he has visited them, has defeated sin, death and the grave, and offers restoration to their original God-given purpose of glorifying him (Ephesians 2 v 1-10). Our outposts are embassies. We communicate the message of the King to the world that belongs to the King.

Second, we have been told to illuminate the kingdom to the world. In our lives, we show what the kingdom is like. Jesus said that the kingdom of God is good news for the poor, the captives, the blind (Luke 4 v 18). So, to the extent that we go into the world as healing agents—renewing, cultivating, restoring—we show the world a glimpse of the future kingdom of God.

Few have thought about this more than Andy Crouch, former executive editor at *Christianity Today* and author of several books, including his masterful work *Culture Making*. He wrote in a blog of how...

"The entire story of God's people—beginning with Abraham and Sarah, and now extending to all nations through the reconciling power of the Cross—is a vast, world-historical rescue mission to restore the capacity for true image-bearing ... to place ourselves at particular risk on behalf of the victims of idolatry and injustice. In every society, Christians should be the most active in using their talents on behalf of those the society considers marginal or unworthy. In every place where the gospel isn't known, Christians should be finding ways to proclaim Jesus as the world's true Lord and 'the image of the invisible God.'" [16]

Do you see the dual mission: to both communicate the good news of the gospel message and to go out into the world and illuminate, through our acts, the good news of the kingdom of God?

This kind of kingdom lens helps us move beyond the perennial and tiresome debates between the "social gospel" and gospel proclamation. They are intrinsically linked. Jesus offered, in his words and deeds, a picture of what his kingdom will look like when it comes in full; *and* he was also very concerned with who gets in and who is shut out of the kingdom.

Jesus doesn't allow us to separate gospel proclamation from social activism, as if they are irreconcilable. An activism divorced from Christ's death, burial, and resurrection becomes an impoverished and powerless activism which will advocate for the wrong causes or use the wrong means or simply run out of fuel. And the work of the gospel in bringing sinners to new life and changing sinners to be more and more like Jesus is the fullest expression of dignity for humans.

---

16 "The Three Callings of a Christian," accessed 2.21.18, http://andy-crouch. com/extras/the_three_callings.

Equally, a gospel proclamation divorced from kingdom acts of mercy becomes an impoverished witness, a kind of fire insurance that doesn't reflect Jesus' radical, paradigm-shifting gospel of renewal. If we will not live out the kingdom, why would we expect anyone to listen to the news about its King?

Christ, in his humanity, fully embodies the image of God. We see this in the gospel stories. He fully obeys the Father by taking the cup of wrath. He fully rules over creation by calming the seas and healing the sick. He fully loves his neighbor as himself by coming to serve and not to be served. Jesus, as the fullest embodiment of humanity, reconciling fallen sinners to himself and his kingdom, is creating image-bearers ready to live out their image-bearing purposes. His resurrecting, restoring work in us is preparing us for an eternity of imaging God in perfect reflection of and connection with our Creator.

BOTH-AND NOT EITHER-OR

So it matters that we don't see gospel proclamation and acts of mercy as either-or, but as both-and. Both are implications of the image of God and should not be set against each other. We shouldn't act as if we have to choose between sharing with someone the good news that their Creator has rescued them from the enemy and demonstrating, by our lives of service, the unique dignity they share as God's image-bearers.

When we choose one or the other, we leave a giant, gaping hole in our gospel. When churches, for instance, refuse to apply the gospel to the issues of injustice in the cultures in which they are situated, they essentially baptize the status quo by their silence. This has happened throughout history, from the silent acquiescence of evangelical churches in the American South during the Jim Crow era to the present temptation for pastors to avoid applying Scripture to controversial issues for fear of disrupting the political sensibilities of the congregation.

At the same time, there is always the temptation for churches to only focus on social issues and downplay the more controversial elements of the gospel's good news: a bloody cross, Jesus' exclusive claims to be God, and the Scriptures' teachings on hell and judgment. It is so much easier to simply be the church that feeds the poor and cares for the environment and doesn't address humanity's greatest need by preaching about humanity's greatest problem: alienation from the Creator.

It is precisely the good news of the gospel message—that Christ has defeated sin, death, and the grave and in his death restores us to our original purpose, to glorify God by fully living out our image-bearing purposes—that empowers us to do good in the world. As we are conformed more closely to the image of Christ, we represent his kingdom in the world with our healing, redeeming, creative acts.

We grasp the full and radical nature of the gospel when we stop seeing communication and illumination as two warring Christian camps, and view them both as part of the radical mission of the church, seeing both as results of the personal and cosmic fruits of Christ's inaugurated kingdom. It's as we come into the kingdom, and are changed to become more and more like the King, that we treat others in the way that he did and does—reaching out to the outsider, caring for the weak, welcoming the marginalized, and calling everyone to repent and believe and come into the kingdom, where image-bearing humans are restored to their original glory and purpose.

THE DIGNITY MOVEMENT

But our activism is more than individual Christians doing good deeds. God, in Christ, is not merely calling persons but a people. Our identity as image-bearers requires us to see ourselves as part of God's kingdom, gathered together as the church. There is a reason why Jesus said his presence, via the Holy Spirit, is most powerfully represented when "two or three are gathered (Matthew 18 v 20).

Again, Crouch writes:

> "This image-restoring calling comes with, and requires, a new family: the church. No one can restore the image alone—only a people can do that, mirroring the original creation of human beings as male and female, the divine communion foreshadowed in the words 'let us make,' and the revelation of God as three in one. Whatever our family of origin, the church becomes our 'first family,' bound together in the creative love of the one from whom every family takes its name (Ephesians 3 v 15). And the church is especially for those who, in the twists and turns of a broken world, have lost their human family—widows, orphans, refugees, strangers. They above all are our brothers and sisters, our companions in discovering our new identity in Christ. Our image-restoring calling cannot happen without the church—without each other." [17]

In the last chapter we talked about the perils of getting the biblical idea of the image of God wrong. The church is at its best when it acts as the embassy of God's kingdom. The church is at its most honoring to Christ and most helpful to the world when it applies Christianity's unique vision of human dignity.

---

17 "The Three Callings of a Christian," accessed 2.21.18, http://andy-crouch.com/extras/the_three_callings.

As the early church was emerging from a new movement into a powerful force within the Roman Empire, it was increasingly distinguished by its commitment to the sanctity of human life, caring for the sick and diseased, and resisting infanticide. Part of what made Christianity strange to the rest of the world was its insistence on valuing those considered disposable by the rest of society. Historian Kyle Harper says that it was early Christian witness that even created an entirely new category for the poor. He writes:

> *"The entire gospel was reduced to the command to love other humans, enjoining not just acts of beneficence but a wholly transformed stance toward the value of others."* [18]

Bishop Gregory of Nyssa, writing in the fourth century, used his office and his influence to apply the language of the image of God to the practice of slavery:

> *"What price did you put on ... the likeness of God? ... Who is his seller? To God alone belongs this power; or rather, not even to God himself. For his gracious gifts, it says, are irrevocable (Romans 11 v 29) ... God does not enslave what is free."* [19]

Gregory's brother, Basil of Caesarea, similarly applied the biblical language of human dignity to force much-needed reforms against sexual exploitation. The fact that these men were standing against the cultural tide when it came to slavery and sexual exploitation fifteen centuries ago shows both that the outworkings of sin change little over time and also that when Christians are seized by the biblical vision of human dignity, it has a dramatic impact on the rest of society.

---

18 Quoted in Shah and Hertzke, *Christianity and Freedom: Volume 1, Historical Perspectives (Law and Christianity)*, page 140.

19 Stuart George Hall, *Gregory of Nyssa: Homilies on Ecclesiastes: An English Version with Supporting Studies* (Walter de Gruyter, 1993), page 74.

Consider William Wilberforce's tireless crusade to end the slave trade. Wilberforce grounded his abolitionism in Christian theology and pushed British evangelicals to consider the human dignity not only of the slave but also of the poor and the marginalized. It is no coincidence that this was also an era when the powerful stopped mocking Christians and the people flooded into the churches. American abolitionists used the Bible's language of human dignity to fight slavery and Martin Luther King Jr., a century later, thundered from American pulpits about the image of God and the dignity of the minority.

Historically, it has been God's people who have established hospitals, built and staffed medical missions, and championed the rights of people who are being oppressed. A church that moves toward the vulnerable, using its power and influence on behalf of those who have seen their dignity ignored or denied, becomes a powerful witness to the nature and reality of the kingdom of God.

A CHURCH OF DIGNIFIED MISFITS

As we demonstrate the kingdom of God by standing up for the dignity of the oppressed, we also embody the upside-down nature of the kingdom of God by displaying the full dignity of humanity within our churches themselves.

This is what Jesus was teaching his disciples in Matthew 20, when, overhearing some of their pitched jockeying for positions in what they thought would constitute Jesus' new kingdom, the Lord reminded them that the kingdom of God is vastly different than the kingdoms of this world. The last, Jesus said, would be first. "Whoever would be great among you must be your servant" (v 26)—for the King of this kingdom himself "came not to be served but to serve" even unto death (v 28).

God's people are always tempted, in every age, to adopt the dignity-denying ethos of the surrounding culture. We always want to align ourselves with the norms of those around us rather than the counter-cultural ones of the kingdom to which we belong and whose King we name as our Lord. This is why it is always easier to spot the mistakes of the church in other cultures and times than ours. Paul rebuked the church in Corinth for hero worship of those with social status or rhetorical gifts by reminding them that when they were called into the kingdom, "not many of you were wise according to worldly standards, not many were powerful, not many were of noble birth" (1 Corinthians 1 v 26). James challenged the churches he wrote to not to treat the wealthy better than the impoverished, as though they were in some way better, for "God [has] chosen those who are poor in the world to be rich in faith and heirs of the kingdom" (James 2 v 5).

The President of the Ethics and Religious Liberty Commission, Russell Moore, reminds us that:

> *"It should not surprise us that the spirit of every age seeks to define human worth in terms of power and usefulness, while the gospel of the kingdom defines human dignity in strikingly different terms, as Christ himself identifies himself not with the powerful but with the vulnerable."* [20]

To fully reflect the biblical view of human dignity in our churches means we not only extend ourselves on behalf of those to whom the world has denied worth, but also that we embody an other-worldly view of dignity in the way we conduct ourselves as a body. It means we resist the world's definitions of worth and power. It means we see a child with Down syndrome as a fully valuable member of

---

20 Russell Moore, *Onward: Engaging the Culture Without Losing the Gospel* (B&H, 2015), page 112.

our body. It means we resist the urge to put on our platforms only those who fit the cultural definition of beauty or masculinity. It means we are the one, and perhaps the only place in society where you are accepted and loved not because of what you can contribute but because of who you are in Christ.

Those who are disabled, those who are poor, those who might not neatly fit into our modern notions of success should have a prominent place in our assemblies, not simply because they have full human dignity as image-bearers of God but because each one is a future king or queen of the universe who will one day reign with Christ (Matthew 19 v 28; Revelation 3 v 21).

Our churches should be collections of people that you would not normally see together. Just imagine congregations filled with people who have no business being together, other than because they are redeemed people of God. Imagine rich and poor, conservatives and liberals, blue collars and white collars and no collars. Imagine a parking lot with hybrids and pickups. Imagine a church lobby filled with walkers and strollers, canes and car seats, tattoos and bow ties. Imagine a church comprising people whose primary and sometimes only commonality is their allegiance to the gospel of Jesus Christ.

We should long for this in our churches, but more than that, we should each ask ourselves what we are doing to make it more of a reality. This begins with each of us accepting—no, celebrating—the upside-down nature of the kingdom. It begins with each of us applying the kingdom ethics of dignity and service within our own hearts—so that we see others as made in God's image, and so serve others because we wish to cultivate their humanity and promote their dignity rather than because we wish to cultivate our ambition and promote our reputation. It begins with treating others with the dignity that the Lord Jesus did, and does, and will.

It's easy for me to advocate on behalf of the vulnerable outside my window, to be stirred by the images I see on social media, to fire off a tweet, to even write a check to a worthy organization. It's much harder for me to love the person next to me in the pew on a Sunday. But it starts there. It's much harder for me to embody servant-hearted love in the way I treat those who work under me and around me. It's much harder for me to celebrate ordinary faithfulness rather than gravitate toward the famous and the beautiful and the talented.

We need a church that smells like Jesus. We need a church that communicates the gospel of the kingdom *and* illuminates the ethics of the kingdom. We are not like the world. We need a church that rejects the tribalizing ethos of the culture around us. We are subjects of another King and we are citizens of another kingdom—a kingdom of dignity and humanity.

4. I AM A MAN
RACE AND THE NATIONS

"Injustice anywhere is a threat to justice everywhere. We are caught in an inescapable network of mutuality, tied in a single garment of destiny. Whatever affects one directly, affects all indirectly."

MARTIN LUTHER KING JR.

In April 1968, Martin Luther King Jr. helped organize a protest in response to unequal treatment of sanitation workers in the city of Memphis. In a city consumed by racial tension, where minorities experienced the crushing indignities of Jim Crow, men lined the streets with sandwich boards bearing the message, "I am a man."

King's was a modest request: can people of color be seen, by the white majority, as humans? They were essentially appealing to their God-given dignity. *I am not an other. I am not less than human.*

I am a man.

Racism focuses on the "otherness" more than on the "man." It is elevating "my people" above "the other people." It is the sin of individual pride writ across a larger canvas. It ascribes greater value to one group of image-bearers than another; it divides up groups of image-bearers according to the way they look or the history they have experienced or the culture they have created, as though these things are more fundamental to who we are and who "they" are than being made in God's image. Racism is often driven by a fear of the "other," but is rooted in an evil that usurps God as Creator and denies the humanity of our neighbors.

No one (well, almost no one) likes to identify as being racist. But the truth is that everyone (well, almost everyone) in every place has given in to the temptation to make themselves feel better, or safer, by treating someone who is "other" worse.

I know I have.

Some of you got to this chapter and are breathing a sigh of exhaustion. In my own context in America and in many other places around the world, there are deep racial tensions. I feel this acutely because I get the most spirited feedback when I write on race. White evangelicals keep asking: "Do we have to keep talking about this? Can't we move on? I'm not a racist." I also hear from quite a few Christians of color who express frustration and exhaustion. There is a lot of hurt and pain, especially at the way they often see their concerns dismissed by those same white evangelicals.

To my white brothers and sisters, I want to encourage you to read this chapter and consider why it is critical for us to think well about race: because it is so intrinsically linked to the Bible's view of human dignity and because the Bible so clearly situates racial unity in the gospel story itself.

To my brothers and sisters of color, I want you to know that I've approached this chapter with much prayer and counsel. Frankly, I'm nervous as I write, because, as a white American evangelical, I have not experienced the suffering and indignities of living as part of a minority. I've benefited from the advantages that come from being a white man in a majority-white country.

And to those of you reading in very different societies or cultures than my American one, I hope that, though your context is not the same as mine, you'll be able to apply the principles and maybe some of the practical ideas to your own time and place.

Some of you might read this chapter and be upset, thinking I've gone too far, and I'm too "liberal" in addressing injustices against minorities. Others will read this and be upset that I've not gone far enough. To both kinds of critics, please know that I write this with an open hand and a broken heart and a love for Jesus.

WHAT WE ASK FOR WHEN WE PRAY "YOUR KINGDOM COME"

Here's why Christians must talk about this.

Jesus offered the gospel as something for "all nations" or "all ethnicities" (Matthew 28 v 19). Luke details how, at Pentecost, people were present from "every nation under heaven" (Acts 2 v 5). This means the good news, made possible because of the death, burial, and resurrection of a dark-skinned Middle-Eastern man, is a gospel for every kind of person, everywhere. Jesus is calling together a multi-ethnic people who will one day gather around his throne:

> *And they sang a new song, saying, "Worthy are you to take the scroll and to open its seals, for you were slain, and by your blood you ransomed people for God from every tribe and language and people and nation, and you have made them a kingdom and priests to our God, and they shall reign on the earth."* REVELATION 5 V 9-10

> *After this I looked, and behold, a great multitude that no one could number, from every nation, from all tribes and peoples and languages, standing before the throne and*

before the Lamb, clothed in white robes, with palm branch-
es in their hands.   REVELATION 7 V 9

The presence of "every ... nation," "from all tribes and peoples and languages" around his throne, reflects God's delight in diversity. He is the one who created, from Adam, the variety of tongues and tribes and nations. He is the one who is calling and building a new people in Christ. He is the one who, in Jesus, creates "one, new man" (Ephesians 2 v 15).

This is where we are heading. And when we pray, "Your kingdom come," this is what we are asking for—to be fully realized by our King's return, and to be experienced in our lives and by our behavior as fully as possible as we wait for the King's return.

This is not a liberal or conservative ideal but a reflection of the fullest expression of humanity and of the heart of Christ.

Of course, between Jesus' first coming and his second, the real-world reality of God's work in the world and in the church is often messy and hard and uneven. It has always been so. The early church struggled with race. Paul was forced to address this reality to congregations struggling to unify Jewish believers and Gentile converts. They were seeing the Spirit of God bring people from a variety of nations and cultures. One of the churches Paul planted, in Ephesus, was situated in a busy metropolis and attracted merchants from around the Roman Empire. Paul says this ingathering of people was a feature, not a bug, of the gospel:

> *For he himself is our peace, who has made us both one and*
> *has broken down in his flesh the dividing wall of hostility by*
> *abolishing the law of commandments expressed in ordinanc-*
> *es, that he might create in himself one new man in place*
> *of the two, so making peace, and might reconcile us both to*

*God in one body through the cross, thereby killing the hostil-
ity. And he came and preached peace to you who were far off
and peace to those who were near.* EPHESIANS 2 V 14-17

Paul was speaking here about Jews and Gentiles—a racial
division that was very entrenched, very antagonistic, historically very complex, and as seemingly intractable as
anything we struggle with and labor under the burden of
today. Yet Paul dares to say that in the gospel of Christ,
the dividing wall of hostility has been broken down; and
therefore within the people of Christ, the walls must
always be kept down.

Racial unity is not incidental to gospel witness but a feature of the gospel's work. We are "one new man"—or one
race—and yet we delight in our diversity. The gospel over-
comes suspicion and pride—those barriers to fellowship
and love and unity—yet it refuses to erase our racial identities. God delights in a people made up of the beautiful,
diverse peoples he created in his image and called "good."

LEARNING TO LISTEN

While we are living in this "in-between," how then can
we work to help heal some of our ugly racial divides? For
white Christians like me, it begins, I think, by listening.
Pastor and author Mika Edmondson says that the one gift
we can offer is to "listen with humility, intentionality, and
measure."[21]

Listening can take several forms. It can be as simple
as intentionally cultivating relationships with minority
Christians and hearing their own personal stories. Recently my wife and daughter listened while a wonderful elder
saint spoke of growing up in our community outside of

---

21 The Gospel Coalition, "How White Christians Can Stand in Solidarity with Minority Brothers and Sisters," accessed 1.16.18, https://vimeo.com/217911629.

Nashville in the 1960s, and of riding the bus after de-segregation, escorted by the National Guard, while bot-tles and rocks were thrown at her and her friends as they walked into school. Listening gets us outside of our nat-ural environment and enables us to begin—just begin—to understand the history and pain of others. To be quiet and listen is to recognize the dignity of the one speaking. It says to them, *You are human and you matter.*

Second, we listen by understanding the particular advan-tages we've been given. When I was in college I took a trip to a very poor part of India. I had not traveled much outside the United States. What I saw stunned me. I saw extreme poverty and disease and illiteracy. After a week spent completely immersed in this environment, I flew home with a sense of shame, images of despair embedded in my consciousness. Why, I wondered, did God allow me to grow up with so many advantages while young people my age, around the world, lack the same access to oppor-tunity? I am not smarter or more gifted or more benevo-lent then they. The reason that I have ended up so privi-leged is because of geography.

This access to opportunity is what many people refer to as privilege. This is a loaded word these days, but it is so important to understanding, and healing, our racial divide. As a man in America, I've been given advantages others have not received: access to education, freedom in a de-mocracy, and life in a safe, stable country. What's more, by virtue of being white in a majority-white country, I have been given advantages even over many of my fellow coun-trymen of color.

This doesn't mean I should apologize for being white, but it should give me some context for understanding the ex-periences of those who live in the minority. To paraphrase a common baseball metaphor I often heard as a boy, I should not assume I hit a triple simply because I was born on third base.

Acknowledging my privilege is not about hating myself but about recognizing that because I was born white—because of the pigment of my skin—I've been given certain systemic advantages: advantages that others—because of the color of their skin—have not received.

Pastor Jonathan Leeman acknowledges this:

> *"This is simply a statistical reality. I, as a white man, am less likely to be aborted as a baby, less likely to be born into poverty, more likely to have two parents, more likely to attend good schools because I live in a good neighborhood, more likely to enjoy the social conditions that make law-breaking less likely, more likely to graduate high school and be accepted into college (absent deliberate admissions policies to the contrary), more likely to be hired (all things being equal), less likely to make shop owners feel nervous when I enter, less likely to be handled roughly and invasively by police officers when pulled over instead of being given a friendly warning (as happened the last few times I was pulled over)—the list goes on."* [22]

Jesus said, "To whom much [is] given, of him much will be required" (Luke 12 v 48). There are some in this world who are given much. We should not hesitate to acknowledge this, if it drives us to be grateful for our opportunities and to use them in service of others, rather than allow them to give rise to pride or a sense of superiority. My privilege does not make me any more of a man, or any better as a man, or any more valuable as a human, than my contemporaries who live in minority communities. My

---

22 "More Than Mere Equality: Identity Politics, White Privilege, and Gospel Peace," The Gospel Coalition, accessed 1.6.18, https://www.thegospelcoalition.org/article/more-than-mere-equality/.

privilege does mean I have the responsibility to listen to them, to value them, and to contend for them.

THE RACE ISSUE IS THE CHURCH'S ISSUE

As the struggles of the early church when it spread beyond the boundaries of Judea show, before we understand race as a social problem, we have to first honestly wrestle with it as a church problem. I'm always sobered by the parable of the Good Samaritan in Luke 10. It was, after all, religious people—members of God's people—who refused to see the man laid in the street. He was there. But his pain didn't discomfort the Levite or the priest. They were on their way to perform their religious practices, and went out of their way to avoid him, and blinded themselves to his humanity.

In many ways, those of us who live in the white-majority culture have the luxury of avoiding the injustices of the minority because those injustices do not wound us. Like the Levite, like the priest, we can train our eyes to look past the humanity of those crushed under the inhumanity of racism. (Perhaps it should not surprise us that in Jesus' parable, it was a Samaritan—a member of a despised race—who saw the man and treated him with dignity.) Every Sunday, when white evangelicals gather for worship, we may, sadly, gather only with those who look like us. We forget that our brothers and sisters of color are our brothers and sisters—and that when we pass by on the other side, it is our family who we are ignoring.

I write this from my own context, as a denominational executive in the Southern Baptist Convention, the largest Protestant denomination in America. For those of you who live in other contexts, you might not be as familiar with the struggles and failures of churches in America, but I'm hoping you can learn from our experiences.

I'm proud to be Southern Baptist, a fellowship of churches who have delivered the gospel and have helped to alleviate human suffering around the globe. But we also bear a shameful legacy of racism that still haunts us. We were, after all, the denomination formed in the mid-nineteenth century to protect and provide theological justification to southern slave-owners. I am proud of the great strides we have made, repenting publically of this sin, issuing strong resolutions against racism[23] and white supremacy,[24] and working, albeit slowly, to nurture and sustain minority leadership in our churches and institutions. But we have much work to do, and still much more to repent of.[25]

Yet although our size and our history mean that our problems are, perhaps, more pronounced, this is not just a Southern Baptist problem but a problem within the wider American evangelical movement. With few exceptions, much of our history includes shameful silence or complicity, by white evangelicals, when it comes to the burdens born by our brothers and sisters of color. The Civil War in America ended the practice of slavery, but it didn't bring an end to racism. Sadly, during the 20th century, most white evangelicals were on the other side—let's face it, the wrong side—of civil rights.

LOSING OUR VOICE

This failure has had massive repercussions that reverberate in our own day—not least, we have lost any right to be

---

23 "Resolution On Racism," accessed 9.14.17, http://www.sbc.net/resolutions/897/resolution-on-racism.

24 "On The Anti-Gospel Of Alt-Right White Supremacy," accessed 9.14.17, http://www.sbc.net/resolutions/2283/on-the-antigospel-of-altright-white-supremacy.

25 Two illuminating books document the SBC's struggle with this issue: Alan Cross and William Dwight McKissic, Sr., *When Heaven and Earth Collide* (NewSouth Books, 2014) and Kevin Jones and Jarvis Williams, *Removing the Stain of Racism from the Southern Baptist Convention* (B&H, 2017).

heard. Alan Cross has written persuasively about the loss of the church's moral voice on important issues of dignity, such as unborn human life, human sexuality, and family formation:

> *"The white evangelical church, especially in the South, having sided with the prevailing status quo of Southern culture to promote the Southern way of life, ended up on the wrong side of scripture and also of history ... The church didn't see that it had lost its moral authority because its pews were largely packed with an older generation wanting stability. But the next generation was being lost. It is not that the church was the source of all of the problems in America, but rather, it was not positioned to provide the answers because it had so clearly failed on the race issue, the one area that it could have addressed successfully if it had had the right perspective ... When the church lost its voice, people looked elsewhere."*

Cross envisions a different scenario:

> *"How different would the witness of the church be today if black and white Christians had joined together in the 1950s and '60s and we were united today?"* [26]

We are still reaping the fruits of that generation's sins. Much of today's decline of Christian influence can be traced, not to secularism, but to the failure of significant sections of the church in the era of slavery and segregation. The salt of our witness lost its savor on the altar of racism. Still today, if we speak up about marriage or religious liberty but not about race, why should we think anyone should listen? If we are courageous concerning justice for those who are made in the image of God and

---

26 *When Heaven and Earth Collide*, page 153.

live in the womb (see the next chapter), but silent about justice for those who have been and still are systemically stripped of the dignity that is theirs as image-bearers as they live in our societies, then we should not be surprised to be charged with double standards.

We might be tempted to think that, because we are living in the twenty-first century, somehow we are better or more equipped than those who came before us. Today, racism looks different than it did in American in the 1960s, but that doesn't mean it doesn't exist. It shows up today in systemic injustices that result in police shootings of law-abiding, unarmed black men and women, such as Philando Castile and Tamir Rice and others. Or in the way politicians seem to cultivate racial sentiments. Or in the inequalities in education or incarceration rates (a system can be racist, and it is very hard for those who benefit from that system even to see such systemic racism, and very easy when we do for us to excuse it as neither our fault nor our problem). Or sometimes it is just out in the open, in the rise of neo-Nazi, alt-right, neo-confederate sentiments among young white people around the world. It is also present in some of the ways we talk about immigrants and refugees as unwanted obstacles to our flourishing, which refuse to recognize their humanity.

And perhaps it shows itself in the way that we baptize our own culture's approach to Sunday worship, and instinctively recoil from the expressions of repentance, praise, or preaching that spring from other cultural soils. We appropriate what we like, but we ask those from other ethnic backgrounds to join our churches by fitting in with our norms.

It is not enough for our churches not to be on the wrong side anymore. We cannot stand aloof from what is going on. We are part of it, and the church in two centuries' time must be able to look back on our church and say, *They led on the right side.* As Cole Brown, author, speaker, and church planter, writes:

> *"If we twenty-first-century Americans claim to preach the same gospel as Paul, we must be careful not to settle only for divine reconciliation—as glorious as it is—when God intends for it also to produce racial reconciliation."* [27]

The work of reconciliation, of course, is hard and messy and looks different in different contexts, but almost always it starts with listening, involves repentance, and demands lament (on behalf of the oppressed and downtrodden, even when—especially when—that does not include us). At times it seems nearly impossible, given the thick tension in our communities. That's why only a gospel-fueled ethic will do. We must believe that if the fledgling movement led by a resurrected itinerant Middle Eastern rabbi could unite Jew and Gentile in the first century, it can unite those divided by racism, suspicion, and hurt in the 21st.

REACHING OUT AND REPENTING

Even as I write and you read this chapter, with your social-media feed full of the latest tensions and injustices and side-taking and name-calling, the temptation is to be paralyzed by fear or a sense of powerlessness and, like the priest and Levite, pass by on the other side. What would it look like to be the Good Samaritan in our moment, in your culture? What can ordinary Christians, in our own unique contexts, do to work for racial unity?

First, we have to be committed to it—not just as a way of virtue-signaling online or sounding compassionate at dinner

---

27 "How Much Should a Gospel-Centered Christian Talk About Race?", accessed 3.27.18, https://humblebeast.com/how-much-should-a-gospel-centered-christian-talk-about-race/.

parties, but really committed. For too long we've considered racial reconciliation a kind of an "a la carte" feature of the Christian life. For those of us who preach, teach, and write, we should look for the many ways the Bible speaks to these issues and be unafraid to offer real-world application. It means intentionally platforming minority voices, working to place more minorities in positions of real authority in our churches, and using whatever influence and power we have to support and sustain young minority leaders.

For those of us (and this is all of us) who hang out, share wisdom with, and pray with Christian friends, it must mean a willingness to listen humbly, to challenge ourselves and others, and to change. It must mean a willingness to embrace multi-ethnic church in a way that is not just a cipher for welcoming folk from different backgrounds into our midst as long as they behave as though they come from our background. It must mean a willingness to proactively seek bridges over which love and truth can travel and with which unity can be built.

One initiative that has gained some traction is the "Sunday Solutions" idea created by US Senators Tim Scott and James Lankford. Scott is African-American and Lankford is white. They have modeled their idea and now encourage ordinary people to gather, one Sunday a month, for a meal with someone who does not look like them, to think through and discuss experiences and differences. Imagine if churches championed this kind of intentional community, urging their people to meet and befriend across racial and political lines, and then letting this spill out of our church memberships and into building bridges within and among our local communities?

Imagine if you did this a couple times a month. That would be a quiet revolution that won't make the news, but may make for real change.

And it also means thinking the best of each other and hoping for the best in each other, by being slow to grow angry with one another and quick to forgive one another, for this is what love does (1 Corinthians 13 v 4-7). I am grateful for the way mentors and friends who look different than me but believe the same as me have patiently discipled me, resisting the temptation to shame me for my lack of awareness. I remember, particularly, a black brother in college, who patiently and slowly helped correct my thinking. He could have given up on me or gotten angry with me. My guess is that I was not the first white person whom he had gently rebuked. He could have talked down to me. Instead, he kindly led me to repentance.

In our discussions on race, let us call each other to repentance when we need to, having removed the planks in our own eyes before we do. But let us not assume the worst in those with whom we are engaging. Oftentimes we are too quick to divide from those whose mission we share and whose goals we laud, simply because we would go at a different pace, or with different priorities, or use different language, or take a different route. Let's see each other's humanity and treat one another with dignity, even when we, or they, fall short.

LIVE IN THE DISCOMFORT

Not long ago, as I was working through this chapter, I had a conversation with an African-American pastor in my denomination. He has become a dear friend who, in the past few years, has endured despite much discouragement. I confessed to him my own distress about the state of race relations and he said to me a word of mild rebuke that continues to roll around in my mind. "Dan," he said, "You need to learn to live in the discomfort."

Live in the discomfort. That is, don't ever get comfortable with a reality where we divide along racial or tribal or any other lines. But don't give up. Don't think you can't make any difference. Be willing to take a risk. This is what the Good Samaritan did as he pushed past cultural biases and entered into the life of the man on the side of the road. Are we willing to lay our lives down, to use whatever influence we have, to recognize the dignity of our neighbors and seek their good?

We know that until Christ returns to fully restore and renew all things, we will never see Christian unity in its fullest richest expression. We will never see complete and total justice. But we can work for it, even as we fall short of it, because we know that one day we will experience it.

What gives me most hope is not, however, in our feeble work, but in the simple rhythms we experience in church life, particularly as we celebrate the Lord's Supper. Every time we lift the cup to our lips, we celebrate the death of a Savior whose blood was spilled for people from every nation and tribe; every time we lift that bread to our mouths, we celebrate the broken and then resurrected body of our Lord. This is happening, every Sunday, in congregations around the globe, from Paris to Peru, from Denver to Denmark, from Harlem to Havana. This sacrament envisions the great feast we will share one day, as brothers and sisters in the Lord, as God finally completes his work of bringing his fractured and divided body together, and his whole multicolored bride dines with him at the King's table. How we long for this day!

5. THE LITTLEST PEOPLE
THE START OF LIFE

"This is a debate about our understanding of human dignity, what it means to be a member of the human family, even though tiny, powerless and unwanted."

HENRY HYDE

It happened, as these things do nowadays, via Instagram. In February 2017 pop star Beyoncé announced that she and her husband, Jay Z, were expecting twins:

"We would like to share our love and happiness. We have been blessed two times over. We are incredibly grateful that our family will be growing by two, and we thank you for your well wishes." [28]

And the whole world rejoiced and marveled at the two lives growing inside of one of the most instantly recognizable people on the planet.

Similar fanfare greeted Catherine, Duchess of Cambridge, when Kensington Palace announced, in August 2017, that she and Prince William were expecting their third child.

---

28 https://edition.cnn.com/2017/06/18/entertainment/beyonce-babies/index. html. Accessed 2.5.18.

In the most-liked post in Instagram history, Beyoncé posed with her hands caressing her stomach and referred to "three hearts." Her mother referred to her daughter's excitement at the prospect of meeting her "babies."[29] Yes. Babies. With hearts. Similarly, news outlets, reporting the pregnancy of Catherine, Duchess of Cambridge, referred to her "baby" (without the scare quotes).

No one thought to refer to Beyoncé's baby as a fetus.

No one suggested that Catherine was not carrying a future prince or princess, but merely a clump of cells that may one day become a prince or princess.

This natural, unfiltered euphoria over these famous babies seems to show how we really think about the unborn. We know instinctively that what is growing inside of a pregnant woman is a future life. And if we really believe Dr. Seuss's words that a person is a person, no matter how small, we have to marvel, then, at the smallest of persons: the mysterious union of sperm and egg that forms a living soul. And we are forced to lament the reality that many of these small persons will never have the chance to experience life, because they have become victims of legalized abortion on demand.

BENEATH THE CROSS

If you are reading this and have gotten to this part of the book, perhaps you are letting out a bit of a sigh. *He is going there, isn't he?* Abortion is one of the most contentious issues in modern life. In America, it has divided the two major political parties for half a century.

I am, as you likely discovered through my work or my writing or just discerned when you read the bio on the back of this book, pro-life. I see the baby in the womb,

---

29 https://www.thesun.co.uk/tvandshowbiz/3644531/tina-knowles-pregnant-beyonce-babies/, accessed 2.5.18.

no matter how small, as a human, with God-given dignity and worth. But I understand that decisions to terminate a pregnancy are fraught with complexity and difficulty, and I realize that some of you reading this might not hold the same position as I do. If that is you, then I ask and hope that as you read through this chapter, you will be willing to try to understand the concerns that animate my support for the baby in the womb.

And let me say at the outset that, as strongly as I believe in justice for the unborn, I believe in grace for those who have made the decision to terminate a pregnancy. I have not been a part of making that kind of choice—but I have sinned in many ways against God, and I, too, deserve his judgment.

Thankfully, like anyone who calls upon his name, I can stand beneath the cross of Jesus and receive fresh mercy and grace. Everybody—everybody—is in need of mercy. Anyone—anyone—who comes to Jesus receives it. "God so loved the world, that he gave his only Son, that *whoever* believes in him should not perish but have eternal life" (John 3 v 16, my italics).

Let me also say that (as we'll be seeing through the rest of this book) the womb is by no means the only place where human dignity is under assault. Many other vulnerable people—minorities, immigrants, the poor—are harmed by unjust systems of oppression. But still, is it possible to talk about human dignity and justice for the vulnerable among us if we are unwilling to wrestle with the questions of life and death that arise when we consider the humanity of society's smallest people?

LIFE BEGINS AT...

The Bible is very invested in the beginning of human life. In one particularly arresting passage, King David, Old

Testament Israel's greatest monarch, muses about his own conception:

> *For you formed my inward parts; you knitted me together in my mother's womb. I praise you, for I am fearfully and wonderfully made. Wonderful are your works; my soul knows it very well. My frame was not hidden from you, when I was being made in secret, intricately woven in the depths of the earth. Your eyes saw my unformed substance; in your book were written, every one of them, the days that were formed for me, when as yet there was none of them.*
>
> PSALM 139 V 13-16

David uses several important descriptors to describe the mystery of conception.

First, notice his recognition of the personhood of the unborn. "You knitted me together." David didn't say, "You knitted it together." Later he says that "I" (notice the personhood) was being "made" and "intricately woven." Even when describing the mass of cells and tissue, David is not impersonal. "My unformed substance" recognizes the humanity of the baby at the earliest possible stage. David was David when he was in the womb just as much as he was David when he was on the throne.

Second, David declares the growing child to be "wonderful" and "fearful." There is a beauty and awe in the creation of a new life. David is echoing God's words at the creation and seeing the development of human life for what it is: good and beautiful.

Third, David credits the work of creating a child, the product of a man and women coming together in sexual intimacy, to God. "You formed" and "you knitted," he says to the Creator: these are "your works." God is present at the conception of every child. He is active in the creation of every child. No matter how small the human, God forms. God sees. God knows.

The Bible assigns the God-endowed dignity of full personhood to the smallest of humans. Consider also the way in which God describes the birth of the prophet Jeremiah:

> *Before I formed you in the womb I knew you, and before*
> *you were born I consecrated you; I appointed you a prophet*
> *to the nations.*   JEREMIAH 1 V 5

God is saying to Jeremiah, *I knew you before you were born and I formed you as you were born.* Jeremiah wasn't the accidental gathering of a blob or a clump of cells, or merely the result of sexual intercourse. Jeremiah was a person when he was at his smallest. So was the unborn John the Baptist:

> *And when Elizabeth heard the greeting of Mary, the baby*
> *leaped in her womb. And Elizabeth was filled with the*
> *Holy Spirit.*   LUKE 1 V 41

John the Baptist, in the womb of his mother, Elizabeth, gave a perfectly human response to the news of the conception of the Christ child. He leaped, inside the womb. He responded to external stimuli.

In all this, the Bible does not shrink from the difficulty of childbirth for the mother. In fact, that pain and cost lie at the heart of the Christian story. Every Christmas we celebrate the virgin birth of Jesus, but we so easily forget that we are reading about the hard and costly pregnancy of an unwed mother, which was sure to bring shame and disrepute on Mary. Joseph, her fiancé, was being called to care for a child not his own. But throughout this entire narrative, there is always an overwhelming sense that this Jesus, even in his earliest and most vulnerable fetal form, possessed full humanity:

The angel said to her, "Do not be afraid, Mary, for you
have found favor with God. And behold, you will conceive
in your womb and bear a son, and you shall call his name
Jesus. He will be great and will be called the Son of the
Most High. And the Lord God will give to him the throne
of his father David, and he will reign over the house of
Jacob forever, and of his kingdom there will be no end."

LUKE 1 V 30-33

Notice how the angel refers to this unborn child with personal pronouns. "He will be great," "his father, David," "he will reign," "his kingdom." Jesus, as an embryo, from the moment of conception, was Jesus—not a potential human, but a person.

This intentional biblical language, from King David to Jeremiah to John the Baptist to Jesus, tells us something about how much beauty and dignity God assigns to the least developed human forms of life. The personhood of a baby in the womb is not based on parental pleasure at their conception, any more than the personhood of a one-year-old is based on parental pleasure at their birth. It is not contingent upon whether their mother is in a good position to take care of them, any more than for a three-month-old or a three-year-old. A person is a person, no matter how small, because they have an inalienable, unceasing, God-given dignity.

"A MEMBER OF OUR SPECIES"

But it's not simply a Christian argument that the unborn baby is indeed a human being. Technological advances such as ultrasound scanning and research on fetal development tell us a similar story.

We now know that the developing embryo is indeed an individual human being, with their own unique DNA, set of chromosomes and genetic blueprint.[30] Dr. Micheline Mathews-Roth of Harvard Medical School says:

"It is scientifically correct to say that an individual human life begins at conception, when egg and sperm join to form the zygote, and this developing human always is a member of our species in all stages of its life." [31]

A baby's heart begins to beat at eighteen days and is pumping blood within twenty-two days. Beyoncé, mourning a miscarriage in 2013, acknowledged the connection between mother and baby: "There's no words that can express having a baby growing inside of you," she said at the time. She also recalled hearing the baby's heartbeat, saying that it "was the most beautiful music I ever heard in my life."[32]

Babies in the womb react to touch; they have detectable brainwaves at six weeks and develop unique fingerprints around nine or ten weeks.[33] New technologies show that unborn babies may react to visual stimuli.[34]

This should cause us to pause and think about what is happening during an abortion procedure. A human life, with a heartbeat and fingerprints and the ability to recognize facial stimuli and sound, is extinguished. Moreover, multiple studies show that at the earliest ages, perhaps as early

---

30 See "Appendix | Prenatal Overview," accessed 9.7.17, http://www.ehd.org/dev_article_appendix.php.

31 "Cetrulo_08.pdf," accessed 9.7.17, http://www.uffl.org/pdfs/vol18/Cetrulo_08.pdf.

32 "Beyoncé's Grammy Awards Performance With Her Unborn Twins Praised for Its Pro-Life Theme," LifeNews.com, February 13, 2017, accessed 1.16.18, http://www.lifenews.com/2017/02/13/beyonces-grammy-awards-perfor-mance-with-her-unborn-twins-praised-for-its-pro-life-theme/.

33 Kristi Burton Brown, "12 Amazing Facts That Prove the Preborn's Humanity in the First Trimester," Live Action News, March 3, 2016, accessed 1.16.18, https://www.liveaction.org/news/12-amazing-facts-prove-preborn-humani-ty-first-trimester/.

34 Vincent M. Reid *et al.*, "The Human Fetus Preferentially Engages with Face-like Visual Stimuli," Current Biology 27, no. 12, June 19, 2017.

as sixteen weeks, a pre-born baby feels pain.[35] Ironically, surgeons are increasingly performing surgery on unborn children and even, at times, applying anesthesia to help numb their pain, while in another section of the same medical facility other doctors are ending the lives, through abortion, of babies in similar stages of development.

Even many who vocally advocate for abortion are having a harder time denying the reality of life inside the womb. Naomi Wolf, feminist and ardent defender of abortion rights, wrote in an essay:

> *"Clinging to a rhetoric about abortion in which there is no life and no death, we entangle our beliefs in a series of self-delusions, fibs and evasions ... We need to contextualize the fight to defend abortion rights within a moral framework that admits that the death of a fetus is a real death."* [36]

Supreme Court Justice Anthony Kennedy acknowledged that what happens in an abortion procedure is indeed a death:

> *"The fetus, in many cases, dies just as a human adult or child would: it bleeds to death as it is torn from limb to limb."* [37]

In a compelling and commendably honest piece written after the release of a series of undercover sting videos that shed light on practices in some parts of the abortion industry, pro-choice columnist Ruben Navarrette admitted that he didn't know if he could defend the legality of abortion any more:

---

35 "Fetal Pain: The Evidence," accessed 2.21.18, http://www.doctorsonfetalpain. com/wp-content/uploads/2013/02/Fetal-Pain-The-Evidence-Feb-2013.pdf.
36 "Re-Thinking Our Pro-Choice Rhetoric," *The New Republic* (Reprinted by Priests for Life), October 16th, 1995.
37 Stenberg v. Carhart, 2000.

"After all this, I still consider myself pro-choice, as I have for the last 30 years. I staked out this position during my freshman year in college. Even then, I understood the abortion debate was a tug of war between competing rights— those of the mother versus those of an unborn baby. I sided with the mother. And I tried not to think about the baby...

"As I've only realized lately, to be a man, and to declare yourself pro-choice, is to proclaim your neutrality. And, as I've only recently been willing to admit, even to myself, that's another name for 'wimping out.'

"At least that's how my wife sees it. She's pro-life, and so she's been tearing into me every time a new video is released. She's not buying my argument that, as a man, I have to defer to women and trust them to make their own choices about what to do with their bodies. To her, that's ridiculous—and cowardly:

"'You can't stand on the sidelines, especially now that you've seen these videos,' she told me recently ... 'These are babies that are being killed. Millions of them. And you need to use your voice to protect them.'" [38]

It is this incontrovertible fact—the reality of the person-hood of the unborn—that compels us to see abortion not as a mere political issue but as a justice issue. If the baby inside the womb is a person at the earliest stages of life, isn't it incumbent on us to advocate for the dignity of these most vulnerable members of our society? As Ruben Navarrette's wife puts it, to use our voice to protect them? Can we really contend that in this "tug of war between competing rights," the claimed right of one person to have

38 "I Don't Know If I'm Pro-Choice After Planned Parenthood Videos," accessed 1.16.18, http://www.thedailybeast.com/i-dont-know-if-im-pro-choice-after-planned-parenthood-videos.

the kind of life they had hoped for is more important than the right of another person to have a life at all?

900,000

This fight for justice seems daunting. In the United States alone, nearly 60 million abortions have taken place since the Roe v. Wade Supreme Court decision legalized abortion in 1973. Over 1.5 billion abortions have taken place around the world since 1980. Though abortion rates in the US are dropping, still every year nearly 900,000 take place.

If we believe each of these are persons, created in the image of God, then we must first weep over a culture that considers their lives so worthless that they can be so easily discarded. We must lament our inability to find a home for the unwanted. And we must examine the way we use language to seek to justify what we are doing. Even the word "abortion" is a euphemism that masks what is actually taking place when a baby is extracted from a mother's womb and deliberately killed. Mike Cosper, writing of the way we politely discuss the taking of innocent human life, says we have...

> *"imbibed a ... disenchanted language that looks at bodies and refuses to assign them any meaning beyond being 'products of conception.'"* [39]

It is even more sorrowful to consider that the abortion industry disproportionately targets the most vulnerable. For instance, a high percentage of babies diagnosed with Down syndrome are aborted, often with the encouragement of those in the medical profession, so that parents can escape the risk of parenting a child with special needs.[40] Iceland

---

39 "The Banality of Abortion," accessed 2.21.18, https://erlc.com/resource-library/articles/the-banality-of-abortion.
40 "PubMed Entry," accessed 9.7.17, http://www.ncbi.nlm.nih.gov/pubmed/10521836.

recently boasted of "eliminating" Down syndrome—in reality, the boast was of eliminating babies with Down syndrome.[41] This kind of elimination of disabled children reflects a view that societies only want, and parents have the right only to choose, the most fit, most desirable children, as if Down's kids do not fully possess dignity and worth. Charlotte Fien, who has Down syndrome, recently testified before the United Nations and pleaded:

> *"We are still human begins. Human beings. We are not monsters. Don't be afraid of us. We are people with different abilities and strengths. Don't feel sorry for me. My life is great ... Please do not try to kill us all off."*[42]

Also disturbing is the way abortion providers like Planned Parenthood seem to target predominantly minority populations. In the US, women of color are five times as likely to have an abortion.[43] Abortion kills black children at three times the rate of white children.[44] There are a variety of factors that lead to this reality, but among them is the intentional placement of abortion clinics in high-minority population centers.

If we believe that each human life was created, knit, in the womb of a mother by a loving Creator, we must be compelled to look past the euphemisms and champion human life in its most vulnerable state. Where others speak of a fetus, a clump of cells, we have to say, we must say, "There is a person there."

---

41 "Down Syndrome in Iceland: CBS News's Disturbing Report," in National Review, accessed 9.817, http://www.nationalreview.com/article/450509/down-syndrome-iceland-cbs-newss-disturbing-report
42 "Snapshot," accessed 9.7.17, https://www.commentarymagazine.com/politics-ideas/down-syndrome-speaks/.
43 "Abortion's Racial Gap," *The Atlantic*, accessed 9.8.17, https://www.theatlantic.com/health/archive/2014/09/abortions-racial-gap/380251/.
44 "Abortion and Race," accessed 9.8.17, http://abort73.com/abortion/abortion_and_race.

OFF THE SIDELINES

A decision to abort a child does not, of course, happen in a vacuum. A variety of factors, including a lack of adequate resources, can form a perfect storm that leads a woman in distress to choose to end the life of the child within her womb. Economic and social conditions—poverty, family dysfunction, systemic injustices—all contribute to the reality that for many pregnant, unwed or unsupported women, there simply seems to be no other choice but abortion. They face an uncertain future, with little or no financial support, and (in some communities) the deep shame of living as an unwed mother.

So it is not good enough for us to claim we are pro-life simply by standing on the sidelines and shouting about abortion every four years. At times the pro-life movement has been criticized for having little concern for babies once they are born or for the dignity of the working poor. I think most of this criticism is unfair, given the generosity and good-heartedness of most who call themselves pro-life. Still, we should hear this criticism. We need to get involved, to understand, to help, to be pro-life after birth as much as we are pro-life before birth.

I have been encouraged by the way in which the church is present to help women who are considering an abortion, through ministries such as pregnancy resource centers (PRCs). I've visited many of these centers around the country and I always come away amazed at their effectiveness—particularly the way gifted, compassionate, gospel-centered volunteers love pregnant women and give them encouragement and hope. For many young women, this is the first time they realize that there is an option besides abortion, and that there is a community who stand ready to help them raise their child. The best PRCs not only offer medical services but also help provide important practical resources for their new babies, parenting classes, and counseling. Studies have shown that PRCs are some of the most effective ministries at both lowering the abortion rate, and also at setting up women on a pathway to flourishing.[45]

And yet we can do more to create better conditions to prevent abortion from becoming the first choice for women in crisis. We should consider the ways in which economic structures and health-care policies might work against a culture of life and squeeze the poor or isolated into situations where abortion seems the only option.

We should also open up our homes for adoption, foster care, and other ways in which we can welcome vulnerable and unwanted children. Our churches should be building strong communities around single mothers, around families with children who have special needs, and around post-abortive women who wrestle with guilt and shame. We need churches where women are willing to give the time and emotional energy to guiding young women to become flourishing moms, and where men are prepared to help young men who have become fathers to stand by their family and step up to their responsibilities. We need to speak out, with whatever power and influence we possess, for any marginalized people group whose voices have been silenced.

We should also resist a zero-sum approach. Sometimes the pro-life movement has hitched itself to unsavory politicians and power in a way that allows it to become a mascot for other political causes, even some that deny the dignity of other people, as though if legalized abortion were stopped tomorrow, it would be the end of assaults on human dignity. But this is not a zero-sum game.

---

45 Care Net, "The Truth About 'Crisis' Pregnancy Centers," accessed 9.29.17, https://www.care-net.org/the-truth-about-crisis-pregnancy-centers.

If being pro-life is simply about unthinkingly voting for a political party who oppose legal abortion without considering other issues of justice, if it's about seizing a cudgel every election season, then we must ask ourselves if we are truly pro-life.

To be pro-life is a way of life. It is an approach that moves us to lend our voices, our prayers, our influence, and our resources to come alongside those whose flourishing is being threatened and whose dignity is being assaulted.

PRO-LIFE IS PRO-JUSTICE

And yet, even as we expand our vision of human dignity, even as we remember that to be pro-life means much more than being anti-abortion, we cannot forget unborn lives.

For many young evangelicals, especially those who care about social justice, there is a tendency to be silent about the tragedy of abortion. It seems there is almost an embarrassment about being labeled "pro-life," perhaps because it seems to involve aligning yourself with older generations of activists or allies with whom you (understandably) disagree on other issues or on tactics. To be vocally pro-life is to be, at times, at odds with those who would be allies on other human dignity issues, such as human trafficking, immigrant care, and racial justice.

But this is no reason to turn away from the most vulnerable among us. We should work toward a public witness that is both pro-life when it comes to life in the womb, and pro-life when it comes to these other issues. We must not listen to the lie that we must choose; or that advocating for one area of dignity means we have done our duty and we can ignore other assaults on human dignity. If our notions of justice don't include these least of us—the precious, powerless, defenseless babies in the womb—perhaps it is no justice at all? What other powerless people groups will we then abandon because to stand up for them is costly?

There is an argument that says additional pro-life legislation doesn't always result in a reduction of abortions. Some say they are personally pro-life, but are hesitant to apply that personal belief to public policy. And yes, the effectiveness of anti-abortion legislation is hard to measure—but there is some evidence that these laws do work. For instance, a reduction in federal funding, in some US states, has resulted in less abortions. And the abortion rate nationwide has dropped during the same time period in which many states have adopted restrictive new laws.[46]

And anyway, mere numbers aren't the only reason for us to pass laws against abortion. Laws are also moral statements about what society does and does not value. So—just as we should with other issues of human dignity such as race, violence, sexual assault, and so on—we should hold our leaders accountable to champion policies that recognize the dignity of the vulnerable. The important civil-rights measures passed in the 1960s didn't erase the incidence of racism, but they did enshrine in law protections for minorities—and they made moral statements about the kind of society we would like to see.

LEARNING FROM WILBERFORCE

Of course, laws are only one tool in our fight for dignity for the unborn. A much more important fight is the one for hearts and minds, and this requires us continually to point to unborn babies and declare their humanity.

---

46 Joe Carter, "Do State-Level Anti-Abortion Laws Reduce Abortion Rates?," ERLC, October 29, 2015, accessed 1.16.18, https://erlc.com/resource-library/articles/do-state-level-anti-abortion-laws-reduce-abortion-rates. Carter thoroughly analyzes the effectiveness of laws.

This happens in conversations, in local churches, in public forums and in relationships.

The experience of America suggests that technology allied to effective advocacy has moved the needle of public opinion. Today there is a higher percentage of the population that affirms the dignity of unborn life than in previous generations. But there is still work to do.

Most of our pro-life work won't happen on Facebook or in national forums but in local contexts. Every day there are vulnerable, at-risk, often-young, women who face an uncertain future. Will God's people flow to these situations and demonstrate Christ's love for both mother and baby? Will we invest time and energy in the lives of at-risk women to guide them toward life and help them raise a child and flourish in their parenting? Will we be willing to put our homes where our mouths are, and be open to fostering or adoption?

Will we create cultures in our churches where those who've made the sad choice to end an unborn life find forgiveness and hope in the good news of the gospel? In every community, there are women and men who live with this regret, and who wonder if they can walk into an evangelical church and be welcomed. What would they hear from the pulpit of your church? What would they hear in conversations among church members after the service?

This is costly work. This is tear-stained work. This is difficult work. But if we see what God sees—the dignity of each human life in the womb—it is work we must do. If we love our unborn neighbor as ourselves, we cannot grow weary of fighting for his or her survival. And, when the task seems unwinnable, we can look to previous justice movements for inspiration. Look at the anti-slavery effort led by William Wilberforce in Britain. For most of his life, Wilberforce fought virtually alone, with British public opinion and economic interests ranged firmly against him. He saw setbacks, and he was tempted to despair. But eventually, through prayerful effort, persistent activism, and mobilizing the church, he saw the slave trade in the British Empire outlawed.

We should pray for a similar outcome. This fight may outlast our generation, even as we quietly, sacrificially change some minds before it is too late, care for some children whose mothers acted with courage and at great cost, and extend compassion toward women who made the opposite decision and who need to meet the God who calls all to account but offers forgiveness freely to all.

And one day, perhaps decades, perhaps centuries in the future, may we or our great-grandchildren look back and wonder how a civil society could ever allow the practice of abortion, and honor those who stood against public opinion and economic interests and defended the dignity, indeed the lives, of those who could not fight for themselves. Because we believe that a person's a person, no matter how small.

6. FRENEMIES
JUSTICE SYSTEMS, PRISON, AND IMMIGRATION

"Justice is doing for others what we would want done for us."

GARY HAUGEN

Justice should matter to Christians more than anyone else because we know and we love a God of perfect justice.

Justice is rooted in God's character. God "loves justice" (Psalm 11 v 7). He is "exalted in justice" (Isaiah 5 v 16). God loves justice, and the expression of his justice is his laws, which set the boundaries within which the world can thrive, we can thrive, and God will be glorified. We tend to think of the law as onerous, as something we have to endure, but the Bible describes God's law as good. There was law in Eden, setting the boundaries for flourishing and life (Genesis 2 v 16-17)—so, though some of God's laws assume the presence of sin (for instance, Old Testament laws regarding sexual assault), divine law itself is part of God's very good creation. God's law is not restrictive, but freeing: it is "the perfect law, the law of liberty," which is why we are "blessed in … doing" or keeping it (James 1 v 25).

God's law is given, you might say, so that we could be fully human.

When we grasp this, we come to share David's attitude to God's law: "Oh how I love your law! It is my meditation all the day" (Psalm 119 v 97). We are most human when we live according to the ways God designed his image-bearers to live in the world he created. Scripture presents God's ordering of the world as a good gift for our flourishing.

But God didn't simply establish laws. God also delegated the authority to make laws to humanity, even before the fall, as part of their exercise of dominion over creation. Adam was given dominion, for instance, over the animals to name them and order them. So it is that in Romans 13, Paul asserts that God has granted human governments the authority to create, enact, and enforce laws:

> *Let every person be subject to the governing authorities. For there is no authority except from God, and those that exist have been instituted by God. Therefore whoever resists the authorities resists what God has appointed, and those who resist will incur judgment. For rulers are not a terror to good conduct, but to bad ... For [a ruler] is the servant of God, an avenger who carries out God's wrath on the wrongdoer. Therefore one must be in subjection, not only to avoid God's wrath but also for the sake of conscience.*
>
> ROMANS 13 V 1-5

In a fallen world, the ideal of good government is to oppose evil and promote good. All human rulers will be accountable for the way they used their power, for either good or evil.

In many ways, this was one of the purposes of God's establishing of the nation of Israel: so that, by her fair systems of justice, she might be attractive to other, pagan nations:

Keep [the laws] and do them, for that will be your wisdom and your understanding in the sight of the peoples, who, when they hear all these statutes, will say, "Surely this great nation is a wise and understanding people." For what great nation is there that has a god so near to it as the LORD *our God is to us, whenever we call upon him? And what great nation is there, that has statutes and rules so righteous as all this law that I set before you today?*

DEUTERONOMY 4 V 6-8

God has clear guidelines for what justice in nations should look like. It should show no favoritism, it should give dignity, it should be fair: "You shall do no injustice in court. You shall not be partial to the poor or defer to the great, but in righteousness shall you judge your neighbor" (Leviticus 19 v 15). The law demanded adequate representation of and witnesses against the accused (Deuteronomy 19 v 15), for God announced his hatred of improper justice, where the guilty are set free and the innocent are convicted (Proverbs 17 v 15).

WHEN JUSTICE DISAPPEARS

When justice disappears or is tilted in favor of one group or class, dignity is assaulted. The book of Judges is, among other things, a record of what happens when there is no justice-giving, justice-guaranteeing authority in a state—when "there was no king in Israel [so that] everyone did what was right in his own eyes" (Judges 21 v 25). A quick read through chapters 19 – 21 shows the horrific results of each person making up their own justice system, inevitably imbalanced toward their own favor.

Civil-rights lawyer Gary Haugen, who has investigated human-rights abuses around the world, says inadequate legal infrastructure is one of the primary drivers for poverty and death around the world.[47] Haugen leads International Justice Mission, a Christian organization devoted to using legal means to rescue the 35 million trapped in sex and labor trafficking around the world. Many legal protections we take for granted in the West, even with imperfect justice systems, are simply nonexistent for billions of people in developing countries. Justice and laws, and their impartial enforcement, are vital institutions for human flourishing.

Yet even in the West, where more robust systems of justice exist and the rule of law is generally accepted, though the inequality may be less pronounced it is still present, often tilting the scales of justice against the most vulnerable. To take one simple example: in a system of courtroom advocacy such as exists in the US and throughout Europe, being able to afford the best lawyers improves one's chances of "winning." We should not be so naive as to think that our many protections and freedoms guarantee equal justice for everyone, every time.

Inequality in the justice system was a major concern for the prophets. Amos railed against the injustices either perpetrated or ignored by both God's people and the surrounding nations against the vulnerable (e.g. Amos 2 v 6-7a; 1 v 13-15). Micah was similarly vexed. He communicated God's anger against the powerful who used their positions of power to exploit and consume the vulnerable:

> *Hear, you heads of Jacob and rulers of the house of Israel!*
> *Is it not for you to know justice?—*
> *you who hate the good and love the evil ...*
> *who detest justice and make crooked all that is straight ...*
> *[Israel's] heads give judgment for a bribe...*

---

47 Gary Haugen, "The Hidden Reason for Poverty the World Needs to Address Now," accessed 10.6.17, https://www.ted.com/talks/gary_haugen_the_hidden_reason_for_poverty_the_world_needs_to_address_now.

> *Therefore because of you*
> *Zion shall be plowed as a field,*
> *Jerusalem shall become a heap of ruins.*   MICAH 3 1-2, 9-12

Micah was particularly exercised about the way those who pointed out these gaps in justice were silenced (2 v 6, 11).

We are prone to the same instincts that Micah condemned. We often don't want to hear the truth and would rather hear that everything is fine. But if just laws recognize human dignity, unjust laws deny human dignity. In many contexts, especially in developing countries without robust democratic norms, there is little recourse to alleviating injustices, but in countries where voters have a share in power through voting and representation, it is a duty for Christians to lean in and speak out for laws and systems that better respect human dignity. The idea of justice is not simply a progressive cause or buzzword, but a mandate for God's people, living out our duty to love the vulnerable. Micah's exhortation to "do justice" (Micah 6 v 8) must echo on in the church.

So what are some hallmarks of a just system?

VICTIMS HAVE DIGNITY

Since God is the ultimate just law-giver and Christ is the ultimate judge (Acts 17 v 31), our systems of justice either adequately reflect this justice or they fail to reflect it.

First, a just system ensures penal justice—that is, those who break the laws receive due penalty. This is because victims have dignity. Remember what God told Noah as he left the ark after the floodwaters of God's judgment had receded?

> *Whoever sheds the blood of man,*
> *by man shall his blood be shed,*
> *for God made man in his own image.*   GENESIS 9 V 6

Punishing those who mistreat image-bearers shows that those who bear God's image matter.

Punishing crime is a reflection of the value of the human being who has been wronged. As Haugen has rightly said, the most vulnerable in societies with inadequate systems of justice are treated as less than human because they have no power to defend their dignity and there is no legal infrastructure in place to do this by penalizing bad behavior.

Penal justice also reflects our knowledge of God. "Christ Jesus ... is to judge the living and the dead" when he returns (2 Timothy 4 v 1); and those who have disobeyed him by refusing to believe the gospel command to repent and be saved "will suffer the punishment of eternal destruction, away from the presence of the Lord and from the glory of his might" (2 Thessalonians 1 v 9). God's penal justice on the last day shows that he cares about what happens in his world; as the British pastor Rico Tice says, it demonstrates that God cares about what I do to you, and he cares about what you do to me. Those who escape human justice do not "get away with it"—which is strangely comforting, even if you are not a Christian. All of us, everywhere, long for some kind of final and full justice. Our penal-justice systems should reflect what we know matters to God, and what we know is coming when his Son returns.

Lastly, penal justice actually gives dignity to the perpetrator, by treating them as a human, accountable for their actions. Penal justice says to the law-breaker that they are a real person, not just the sum of their circumstances and their synapses—and that their real choice has consequences, because they are a human and not an automaton.

(By the way, the truth that blood shed fatally is an image-bearer destroyed is why we should not let the increasing incidence of mass shootings in America inoculate those of us who live in the US against the tragedy of the bloodshed. Rather, it must motivate us to work on solutions that reduce gun crime. To some, that last sentence obviously means that we should be pro gun-ownership; to others it means equally clearly that we should be anti gun-ownership. But let's recognize, first, that those who are driven by an honest desire to prevent killings fall on either side of this debate; and second, that we need to be willing to listen to those we disagree with, and allow our own thinking to be open to challenge, rather than assuming we are right each time the debate comes up again. We should not let our partisan preferences blind us to what can be done to ensure safe communities.)

CRIMINALS HAVE DIGNITY

One of my heroes is the late Chuck Colson. Colson, a central figure in the Watergate scandal that took down the presidency of Richard Nixon, was known as the "hatchet man" for his willingness to perform any political dirty trick in order to advance his party's interests. But not long before he was indicted and sentenced to jail, Colson experienced a profound conversion to Christianity.

This was not one of those "jailhouse" conversions made in order to get early release on parole. The gospel turned Colson from a hatchet man into a man of God. And his experience behind bars gave him a deep and abiding love for prisoners. For the rest of his life, until he passed away in 2012, Colson devoted himself to prison ministry and reform of the criminal-justice system.

Prison Fellowship, the ministry launched by Colson, is a living embodiment of the call to Christians in Hebrews 13 v 3 (and the call of Christ in Matthew 25 v 39-40) to remember that prisoners and their families are people. All around the world, trained volunteers go into local, state, and federal prisons, preaching the gospel of hope and healing to the incarcerated. Churches participate in Angela Tree Christmas programs, which deliver Christmas gifts to the children of prisoners.

What many may not be aware of is Colson's lifelong campaign to reform criminal justice around the world. One of his last acts before his death was to secure passage of the Prison Rape Elimination Act in the US Congress, a tough measure that sought to crack down on the sexual assault of prisoners.

Colson advocated justice for victims and implored Christians to see the dignity of the incarcerated. After his death, a bipartisan commission was named by the US Congress to suggest changes to the American criminal-justice system.

Colson saw prisoners as people. A criminal—no matter what they have done—always remains a human (despite what some in the media suggest). Often, they are very broken people; frequently, though responsible for their actions, the circumstances they were born into or raised in have helped shape them in negative ways. A godly justice system recognizes this, and so ought we to as Christians. It is right to be angry with a perpetrator for what they have done, and to call for justice to be done—but it is also right to mourn for them, for the way that the image of God has been so twisted and marred, and to pray for and seek restoration for them.

Today, this may lead us to be concerned about various aspects of our own nations' justice systems. Though the US is home to five percent of the world's population, it has 25% of the world's prisoners.[48] Over 2 million people in America are incarcerated—one out of every 100 adults

---

48 "Responding to Crime & Incarceration: A Call to the Church," page 3, accessed 10.13.17, https://www.prisonfellowship.org/site/wp-content/up-loads/2017/06/Justice-Declaration-White-Paper_FINAL.pdf.

in America is in prison.[49] The UK has also seen an explosion in its prison population, the number of prisoners doubling between 1950 and 1995 and then doubling again between 1990 and today, while the lengths of prison stays have increased by over 30% in the last fifteen years.[50]

You might assume—as I did—that increased incarceration and longer sentences would be the reasons that violent crime and property crime have significantly dropped since their peak in the early 1990s. But researchers have found that longer incarceration rates and increased imprisonment are actually counterproductive to community safety.[51] As well as increased incarceration being only a small factor in reducing crime, it appears that it also contributes to high rates of re-offending by ex-prisoners.

Not only this, but there is a mountain of evidence that our judicial systems do not balance their scales impartially. People of color are stopped and arrested at much higher rates than the rest of the population, and are often given longer and harsher sentences for the same crime.[52] One in 15 black children have a parent in prison, compared with one in 41 Hispanics and one in 100 whites. Michelle Alexander, in a terrific book, calls mass incarceration "the new Jim Crow."[53]

---

49 "One in 100: Behind Bars in America 2008," by Pew Charitable Trusts, accessed 10.13.17, http://www.pewtrusts.org/~/media/legacy/uploadedfiles/pcs_assets/2008/one20in20100pdf.pdf.

50 "Tough Talk on Crime has Led to a Crisis in Britain's Prisons," The Guardian, May 5, 2016, accessed 2.20.18, www.theguardian.com/commentisfree/2016/may/05/tough-talk-crime-crisis-britains-prisons-suicides-assaults.

51 See "Responding to Crime & Incarceration: A Call to the Church."

52 "Police Behavior During Traffic and Police Stops - 2011," from the US Justice Department, accessed 10.14.17, https://www.bjs.gov/content/pub/pdf/pbtss11.pdf; "Federal Sentencing Disparity 2005-2012," from the Justice Department, accessed 10.14.17, https://www.bjs.gov/content/pub/pdf/fsd0512.pdf.

53 Michelle Alexander, The New Jim Crow: Mass Incarceration in the Age of Colorblindness (The New Press, 2012).

"Do the crime, do the time" is not a wrong approach. We need an approach to sentencing that is adequate, punitive, and proportionate. But our view of justice should encompass both the dignity of the victim and the dignity of the prisoner. This is not an either-or.

JUSTICE THAT SEEKS TO RESTORE

This is where restorative justice—a justice that seeks to rehabilitate the prisoner—respects both prisoner and victim. Policies of tougher sanctions and increased incarceration rates seem to do neither. Increased incarceration, especially for low-level crimes, seems to create tougher and harder criminals, who then perpetrate more violence against victims. At times, our prisons become criminal-making factories, where, because of long sentences and poor, inhumane conditions, we create a more violent criminal. Or ex-prisoners are thrust back out onto the street into a world where they find jobs are scarce due to their criminal record, and there are few onramps into a productive life. Crime so easily looks like the only plausible way forwards.

But rehabilitation and restoration, which includes the full range of spiritual, mental, and physical aspects, results in fewer criminals and therefore fewer victims.

Encouragingly, there is growing bipartisan consensus in the United States to change our sentencing laws and establish both robust re-entry programs that give prisoners an onramp into a more flourishing life and new ways of handling misconduct like drug offenses, where offenders are directed to rehabilitation and care rather than jail. This typically involves public-private partnerships and often involves churches and Christian nonprofits, such as Prison Fellowship and other organizations.

This approach is starting to show some real promise. The state of Texas, for instance, radically reshaped their criminal-justice system, reducing the prison population by 12% through sentencing reform and other new approaches. The crime rate has dropped 23%.[54]

Of course there is much more work to be done in America and other Western nations to adopt justice systems that adequately punish the guilty, provide safety for citizens, and work to give dignity and offer restoration to the prisoner. This is a great opportunity for churches to both speak up and help reform the system and to reach out and minister to prison populations in their community. Many churches are already deeply engaged in this work, through educational efforts, job training, mentoring, and Bible study. Some Christian legal-aid groups offer needed legal help for low- or no-income prisoners.

The inescapable question in this discussion is, of course, what should we make of the death penalty? Good, thoughtful Christians have long disagreed on this. Some view giving the state the power to end life as a violation of the truth that all people bear the image of God. Others say that it is precisely because of the very high value of human life—created in the image of God—that the state should have the power to take the life of someone who has taken life (Genesis 9 v 6).

I'm deeply conflicted on this issue. I do believe in the death penalty in practice, based on the above reasons and because the state bears the sword of justice, given by God (Romans 13 v 4). And yet I'm deeply uncomfortable with the way the death penalty is carried out in America, both in terms of the racial disparity and the lack of adequate legal resources for the poor. A few years ago I read *The Innocent Man* by John Grisham—a book about real people

---

54 "Responding to Crime & Incarceration: A Call to the Church," page 9, accessed 2.20.18, www.prisonfellowship.org/site/wp-content/uploads/2017/06/Justice-Declaration-White-Paper_FINAL.pdf.

on death row—and was shaken to the core by the sloppy, unjust way in which prisoners end up facing execution. So while I'm for the death penalty in principle, I'm mostly against it in the way it is carried out.

We should long for a justice that respects the dignity of every human being, both victim and perpetrator, and that more adequately reflects the perfect justice of our Lord, the righteous judge, who will one day come back to establish his perfect kingdom (2 Timothy 4 v 8). We should care about the treatment of prisoners while incarcerated and reject any ethos that sees them as less than human. We should pray for and call for a justice system that is both penal and restorative. How we balance these two priorities will be an aspect of disagreement. But that we should be seeking to balance both of them should not be.

OUTSIDERS HAVE DIGNITY

In the last few years, a rising movement of populism and nationalism has swept Western countries. In America, it fueled the unexpected election of an outsider President. In Britain, it powered the referendum vote to leave the European Union. Across Europe it has upended governments (such as in Austria) and energized independence movements (such as in Catalonia).

In some ways, these populist movements have given voice to peoples who have been left behind—working-class groups who seem punished by increasing globalization. But there is also a dark underside to some of the more extreme elements of this movement, especially seen in some of the ugly rhetoric that has characterized our discussions about immigrants and refugees.

This has happened at the same time as (and, in some cases, partly as a result of) unrest around the world leading to the greatest displacement of peoples in the modern world, creating a refugee crisis that is more massive even than during the post-World-War-II era.[55] Many of these people have been forced to leave their homes and communities and wander the world, trying to find refuge for their families. They are being met, in some prosperous Western countries, with suspicion and anger. In a heartbreaking story about the Yazidi people, forced by ISIS out of their homes in Northern Iraq, journalist Cathy Otten describes a kind of "cold violence," a new level of suffering beyond the violence perpetrated by terrorist groups, that is the result of being displaced and unwanted:

> *"Around the world, a broader kind of cold violence continues. It's the violence of indignity, of forgetting, of carelessness and of not listening. It's there in the way politicians talk about refugees, and in the way the stateless are sometimes written about and photographed by the western media. It's there in the fear of outsiders. It's there in the way humans dismiss other humans as less worthy of protection or care. When cold violence and hot violence merge, we get mass killings inflicted on the most vulnerable."* [56]

Issues of immigration, refugees, and borders are complex issues, of course, and good Christians will disagree on exactly what the right policies should be. And we do acknowledge that Romans 13 gives nation-states the authority to set their own boundaries. But in the debates that continue to rage in Western countries, Christians should resist the Darwinian idea that the flourishing of immigrants is an obstacle to our own flourishing. We should resist the temptation to diminish

---

55 https://edition.cnn.com/2016/06/20/world/unhcr-displaced-peoples-report/index.html. Accessed 2/5/18.
56 "Slaves of Isis: The Long Walk of the Yazidi Women," The Guardian, July 25, 2017, accessed 1.16.18, http://www.theguardian.com/world/2017/jul/25/slaves-of-isis-the-long-walk-of-the-yazidi-women.

the dignity of immigrants. And we should not seek to protect our own living standards at the expense of their lives.

A vision of the kingdom of God changes the way we see the movement of peoples, both through immigration and refugee care. It is amazing how often the plight of the immigrant is central to God's instructions for his people (and, indeed, his descriptions of his people). According to one study, the word *ger*, often translated as alien, stranger, or sojourner, appears ninety-two times in the Old Testament alone.

When I read about the suffering of refugees, when I see the plight of immigrants who try everything to get to prosperous, Western countries, my heart should break.

Should we turn our eyes away from their need? Should we recoil in fear of their moving into our communities? Or should we meet them with the love of Christ, a love which took him to the cross and should see us shouldering our own crosses, too? Some of these displaced families are our own brothers and sisters in Christ, pushed from their homelands and persecuted for their faith. Others are Muslims whose hearts may be open to gospel witness embodied by the hospitality of their hosts. Will they find a church whose gospel is compelling and attractive, or a church that is closed and fearful?

Of course it is prudent and wise for governments to think of the best ways to assimilate refugees, and to protect from terrorism and ways in which their compassion can be manipulated by those who would seek to do harm. But we Christians should be motivated not only by our personal safety but by the love of God. Remember, Jesus said in Luke 12 v 48 that "to whom much [is] given, of him much will be required." As an employed, white, working Westerner, I enjoy much relative prosperity and privilege. Should I be motivated primarily by a desire to keep that to myself or should I be willing to speak out for the welfare of immigrants and refugees, and willing to personally invest time and money to help see them find safety?

It is easy to give in to fear, but the Bible tells us that the movement of peoples and nations is ordained by God:

> *He made from one man every nation of mankind to live on all the face of the earth, having determined allotted periods and the boundaries of their dwelling place, that they should seek God, and perhaps feel their way toward him and find him.* ACTS 17 V 26-27

We can and likely will disagree on the finer points of immigration policy, but we must at the same time be open-hearted and even-handed when it comes to the way we think about immigrants. By holding out a closed fist instead of an open hand to immigrants, we may be missing an opportunity for God to bring revival to a moribund evangelical church. In many communities in America and in Europe, it is the immigrant church that is the most thriving and possesses the strongest gospel witness.

Thankfully, despite the hateful rhetoric we see on social media and cable news, there are examples of churches all over the world opening up their doors and their homes to the displaced. My friend Bryant Wright, pastor of Johnson Ferry Church in suburban Atlanta, has led his people to open up their homes, for instance, to Syrian refugees. In our own community in Nashville, many churches are ministering to Kurdish and Egyptian refugees. Countless Syrians who were allowed into Germany in the summer of 2016 have received both practical help and the gospel of Christ from churches there.

The point is this: whatever a Christian's view on his or her nation's immigration policy, and the extent to which the door should be opened, a Christian's view of immigrants

who do come into their country must be one of an open
heart of compassion.

THE REALITY OF TRAFFICKING

Some—many—of those on the move between countries
are the victims of human trafficking. Some—many—of
those who move of their own free will become victims
of modern slavery when they reach their destination. The
scope of human trafficking is staggering. Consider these
statistics from the International Labor Organization:

- There are 20.9 million victims of human trafficking
  around the world.[57]
- 68% are trapped in forced labor.
- 26% are children.
- 55% are women and girls.
- Human trafficking is a $150 billion industry worldwide.[58]

These numbers seem too big to get our minds around. But they
represent millions and millions of little girls and little boys, enslaved, right now. Each is somebody's child, with hopes and
dreams dashed. Each is a human created in the image of God,
now treated and traded as a commodity in an underground
market. And it is happening where we live. Much of the forced
sex-trafficking happens in our communities, in sex shops and
brothels and nightclubs. It fuels the porn industry.

Thankfully, Christians have awakened to this injustice and
are working both to rescue victims through the work of
organizations such as International Justice Mission (whose
President and CEO, Gary Haugen, I quoted earlier in this

---

57 "New ILO Global Estimate of Forced Labour: 20.9 Million Victims," accessed 10.14.17, http://www.ilo.org/global/about-the-ilo/newsroom/news/
   WCMS_182109/lang--en/index.htm.
58 "Economics of Forced Labour: ILO Says Forced Labour Generates Annual
   Profits of US$ 150 Billion," accessed October 14, 2017, http://www.ilo.org/
   global/about-the-ilo/newsroom/news/WCMS_243201/lang--en/index.htm.

chapter) and to provide other kinds of needed help such as aftercare and mentoring. But there is always more to be done. We need to push our governments to invest more resources in pursuing trafficking networks and to reform the laws to punish the trafficker rather than the prostitute who is often punished even though she or he was being forced into sexual servitude against their will. There is also an opportunity for churches to come alongside victims of trafficking with aftercare and support, helping them transition into a flourishing life in the community.

WHAT CAN WE DO?

So what can Christians do to help create a more equitable justice system? First, we must maintain hope. Justice can be done. Systems do change. We can develop ways of administering justice that provide a glimpse of the final and perfect justice to come in Christ's kingdom. Though he has seen much injustice, Gary Haugen is encouraged:

> *"Almost all criminal justice systems ... start out broken and corrupt, but they can be transformed by fierce effort and commitment."* [59]

For the average follower of Jesus who is not a lawyer or a policy expert, there are still ways in which we can use our resources and influence to bring about change.

We can use our money, our time, and even our houses to come alongside those in need, especially refugees and immigrants in our communities. We can give our money to fund ministries to prisoners such as Prison Fellowship, or to refugees such as World Relief. Organizations like World Relief offer great opportunities to host immigrant families, to help

---

59 "The Hidden Reason for Poverty the World Needs to Address Now," accessed 10.6.17, https://www.ted.com/talks/gary_haugen_the_hidden_reason_for_poverty_the_world_needs_to_address_now.

provide for the displaced, and to advocate. I suspect many of us have not even considered whether we have space and capacity to extend hospitality to those who are in most need of it. But this may be the way we are being called to live out the biblical command to care for the stranger among us (Exodus 22 v 21; Matthew 25 v 35-40).

We can pray, too. It is hard to deny someone's humanity if we are praying for them. Next time you read or hear of a criminal whose behavior you cannot countenance and whose motivations you cannot even comprehend, why not commit to praying for them? Praying for someone reminds us that they are a person, rather than a problem or a prison number.

Lastly, simply commit to being even-handed as you think about complex issues such as immigration and criminal justice. Applying the image of God to those we often view as obstacles to our flourishing can help change the conversation in our churches and our communities. The media tends to present prisoners and immigrants as "other," as "them," as "less"—so we must consciously remember, all the time, that victims, perpetrators, and outsiders are people, made in God's image, and no more or less deserving of his love and his people's kindness than we are.

Remembering this would, I think, change our thinking. It would change our prayers. It would change our conversations. And it would fuel a longing for our societies to reflect, in some small but increasing way, the coming kingdom of our God, whose laws are good and whose justice is perfect.

7. FACING THE FINAL FOE
DEATH, DISEASE, AND HEALTHCARE

"All life is created in the image of God and worth our greatest efforts to preserve and protect, and He alone is the one who should order the length of our days."

JONI EARECKSON TADA

When I pastored my first church, I was not yet thirty. The church was full of people much older than me. Scripture, of course, is chock full of instruction for young pastors to have respect for their more senior brothers and sisters in Christ, and I learned to live this out during my six years at that church.

I sat at bedsides, reading Scripture and praying with sweet saints on their way to glory. I held the hand of people as they breathed their final breath before entering heaven. And I presided over quite a few funerals for both young and old after their lives on earth had expired. As my friend Casey Hough says:

> *"It is in situations like these that a pastor's theological mettle really gets tested. Pastoral care beside the death-bed is holy ground. For, it is here, in the face of certain death, that all of our white-ivory-tower theorizing about*

eschatology looks us in the eyes and asks, 'Are the dead really raised?'" [60]

The Christian story both acknowledges the reality of illness, pain, and death and offers the most radical rebellion against this fierce and cruel enemy. The world was once good and beautiful, created by the intricate design of a loving Creator. But sin has pervaded every aspect of human existence and is the source of disease and pain and death—not specific sins by those who suffer, but sin as the cause of the corrupting decay of a beautiful world. Disease and death don't diminish our dignity, but they are realities that we must contend with.

But this same Christian story tells us that the perfect image-bearer, Jesus Christ, conquered sin and death and the grave, and is renewing and restoring the world. Instead of a desperate and inevitably temporary staving off of ageing and death, Christ offers a completely new world, a new creation, and yes, new and uncorrupted bodies.

In Jesus we have a friend who wept in bitter anger at the death of his friend Lazarus (John 11 v 35). Jesus wasn't flippant about death—death, after all, was the greatest and last enemy that Jesus came to defeat. Death is an assault on the dignity of God's image-bearers. Jesus, as the eternal Son of God, the Creator, reverses the curse and raises the dead to new life.

It is this future hope that enables Christians to endure the pangs of death in this corrupted world, and to walk through hard times with joy rather than seeking to escape them or buckling under them. In our present, broken humanity, we are "jars of clay," says Paul: but we "do not lose

---

60 "And Death Shall Be No More: Confronting the False Gospel of Death with Dignity," ERLC, June 21, 2016, accessed 1.16.18, http://erlc.com/resource-library/articles/and-death-shall-be-no-more-confronting-the-false-gospel-of-death-with-dignity.

heart. Though our outer self is wasting away, our inner self is being renewed day by day" (2 Corinthians 4 v 7, 16). Our mourning over death is met by resurrection hope—with the knowledge that one day we will rise to be with Christ, body and soul. Knowing our present dignity changes the way we look at the brokenness we and those we love now endure, and the way we think about the journey we are all on—the journey toward the end of this life.

A CHRISTIAN VIEW OF DEATH (AND AGE)

Sitting at the deathbed of a friend or loved one forces us to confront serious, existential questions. What is humanity, really? What is eternity, really?

Remember, the Bible teaches that our dignity is bestowed on us by our Creator, not earned or maintained or measured by us through our capacity, or given to us by society.

God gives us our dignity because God is our Maker. Moses wrote that it is God who determines our beginnings and our endings: "I kill and I make alive" (Deuteronomy 32 v 39); and Paul reminds us that it is God who gives man "breath" (Acts 17 v 25). In him, we "live and move and have our being" (Acts 17 v 28). So every life, even a life peering over the precipice of death, has value, measured not by our own sense of dignity, but by God.

This is why we cannot view life—even a life that feels useless, or a life that cannot escape pain, or a life that is dependent on the care and feeding of others—as disposable. God looks at a human in a vegetative state, or a human diagnosed with terminal cancer, or a human with severe and debilitating pain, as completely human and just as precious as someone who is fit, healthy, and happy. In God's economy, the most helpless resident of an assisted-living facility has as much value as the most virile athlete performing at peak performance. Our dignity doesn't leave us when we age, when we grow old and helpless and near death. Every life is valuable and every life is eternal. And death, the last and often most difficult of all trials we face in this earthly life, has been defeated by Christ for those who trust in him.

So we must conclude that the choice about life and death lies in the hands of the Maker, the dignity-giver. My life, whatever stage it is at and however I feel about it, is not my own to take. I am not my own.

This is why Paul could write, from a jail cell, about his peace with God's ownership of his last breath:

> *For to me to live is Christ, and to die is gain. If I am to live in the flesh, that means fruitful labor for me. Yet which I shall choose I cannot tell. I am hard pressed between the two. My desire is to depart and be with Christ, for that is far better. But to remain in the flesh is more necessary on your account.* PHILIPPIANS 1 V 21-24

For the Christian, as for Paul, death is not a disaster but a doorway to a better life with Christ. Christians will lean toward eternity. But equally, for the Christian, as for Paul, there is work to do in this life until the moment God calls time on it and calls us home. Our life is not our own, and in death we will not be on our own. The Christian is, in one sense, always keen to die and "depart and be with Christ," and also more determined to live, in "fruitful labor."

DIGNITY AND EUTHANASIA

We need to recapture this view of death and of life, insisting that it is the Maker—and the Maker alone—who begins and ends life, because we live in a utilitarian culture that increasingly marginalizes the elderly. Aging populations, with diminishing capacity and diminishing perceived social utility, are easy prey for powerful interests.

A recent *New Yorker* investigation revealed a scheme in a Nevada county where elderly couples were forced from their homes and their assets were seized against their wills and without knowledge of their family members.[61] It was dishearteningly easy for nefarious people to sweep in and label elderly folk as wards of the state and appoint themselves guardians, all within a legal framework. Thankfully, changes are being made to Nevada state law, but that it happened at all should be alarming.

Aging populations are also vulnerable to the increasingly powerful "death with dignity" movement. This movement has successfully legalized assisted suicide around the world. Many countries in Europe have especially liberal euthanasia laws. While initially promised as a remedy for terminal patients, it has now been expanded to be offered to any person whose life is considered less than ideal. In Belgium, the country with perhaps the most permissive-assisted suicide laws, assisted suicides are rising even for non-physical, non-terminal cases.[62] In many of these situations, patients do not posses the rational capacity to make decisions along these lines.

Belgium just recently extended euthanasia to children.

Philosopher Miroslav Volf warns of the problems with a state that sanctions and encourages this practice:

> *"A society in which physician-assisted suicide is legal would likely become one in which physician-assisted suicide is expected. Those diagnosed with terminal medical conditions would be seen as selfishly burdening others (the medical*

61 Rachel Aviv, "How the Elderly Lose Their Rights," *The New Yorker*, October 2, 2017, accessed 1.16.18, https://www.newyorker.com/magazine/2017/10/09/how-the-elderly-lose-their-rights.

62 "A Legal Challenge to the European Culture of Death," *Commentary Magazine* (blog), November 10, 2017, accessed 1.16.18, https://www.commentarymagazine.com/politics-ideas/a-legal-challenge-to-the-european-culture-of-death/.

system and their families, in particular) if they didn't request it. [63]

Christians oppose euthanasia for several reasons. We oppose it because we believe, as the Scriptures remind us, that every human life has unique value and worth, regardless of its utility. We oppose it because so often the "death with dignity" industry preys on the vulnerable. We oppose it because it offers cheap promises of hope that are empty, and because we find in the gospel's beautiful story of cosmic and bodily redemption a richer, more real hope.

In 2014, Brittany Maynard went public with her desire to choose euthanasia rather than suffer an excruciating death. It was hard not to sympathize with her choice. Few will suffer the awful end-of-life experience that a cancer of like hers will bring. Having seen dear friends suffer through the crucible of terminal illness, there is a part of me that understands the impulse to do anything to see the suffering stop. But in doing so, we might miss what God is doing.

In response to Maynard, Kara Tippetts, a young mother of four, wrote of her own fight with cancer. A Christian, she urged Brittany to find hope in Christ. In some of her final words, Tippetts wrote to her eloquently:

> *"You have been told a lie. A horrible lie, that your dying will not be beautiful. That the suffering will be too great ... But in my whispering, pleading, loving voice ... will you hear my heart ask you, beg you, plead with you—not to take that pill.*
>
> *"Yes, your dying will be hard, but it will not be without beauty. Will you please trust me with that truth? More importantly, will you hear from my heart that Jesus loves*

---

63 *A Public Faith: How Followers of Christ Should Serve the Common Good,* (Brazos Press, 2013), page 121.

you. He loves you. He loves you. He died an awful death upon a cross so that you would know him today, that we would no longer live separate from him and in our death. He died and his death happened, it is not simply a story.

"He died and he overcame death three days later, and in that overcoming of death he overcame the death you and I are facing in our cancer. He longs to know you, to shepherd you in your dying, and to give you life and give you life abundant—eternal life." [64]

That, I think, is a death with dignity. It is the dignity of someone who knows who has made them, and who seeks his glory and his leading in all circumstances, and who knows that death is not the end and that, in Christ, death will for them be "gain."

STOP ACTING AS IF YOUTH IS BETTER

Knowing every person bears God's image not only informs our approach to euthanasia; it also influences how we treat people who are elderly. God doesn't measure value the way we are so often tempted to measure it—by youth, attractiveness, and physical abilities. There is no season of life that erases the image of God in humans.

The truth is that even those who reject euthanasia are often unwitting evangelists for its arguments. When we prioritize youth and attractiveness and marginalize the elderly, we are communicating a message far different than the Christian gospel.

I recently heard of a church that asked a lead guitarist to stop playing with its main worship team. It wasn't

---

64 "Dear Brittany: Why We Don't Have To Be So Afraid of Dying & Suffering That We Choose Suicide," Ann Voskamp (blog), October 8, 2014, accessed 1.16.18, http://annvoskamp.com/2014/10/dear-brittany-why-we-dont-have-to-be-so-afraid-of-dying-suffering-that-we-choose-suicide/.

because the guitarist's skills had diminished—he is very good—but because his gray hair wasn't "the look we are going for." This church is probably very pro-life and would, if you asked their leaders, be steadfastly opposed to euthanasia. They likely have a robust ministry to the elderly. But they are sending a message that youth is better and that gray hair is the wrong look. But the "look" that the King of God's kingdom is after is one in which young and old, rich and poor, feeble and thriving worship together in weakness. It is, Paul says, often not the impressive who are called, but the weak and the frail (1 Corinthians 1 v 26).

In seeking to reach the next generation, Christian organizations can often project a Darwinian anti-gospel that suggests only the young, the virile, the slender, and the beautiful are wanted. I'm deeply worried about my own generation of leaders. I wonder if, in our zeal to change the world and lead differently, we are guilty of disrespecting those who have gone before. In our desire to take the stage, are we guilty of sweeping our elders off the stage? And for all of us, in our personal, individual interactions, do we dismiss someone because of their gray hair or write off their perspective because it is embedded in experience from a time-period before we were born? Yes, "the glory of young men is their strength"—but "the splendor of old men is their gray hair" (Proverbs 20 v 29). For the Christian, age brings experience, and experience buys wisdom, and wisdom needs a hearing.

Even infirmity brings opportunities. No longer dynamic and independent, we can learn a fresh dependence on others, and supremely upon Christ. And those around the older generation can learn to serve them, sacrificing their own comforts and time to give to another. That is also a step closer to the way we were created to exist.

I saw this firsthand in my own family. My grandfather, once a healthy and robust army veteran who made sacrifices for others and regaled us grandchildren with tales from his time in World War II, spent the last years of his life in an assisted-living facility. I saw my mother visit my grandfather every day of his life until he passed away, caring for him, bringing him what he needed, and talking to him as if he had full, rational capacity. She lived out the meaning of the command to honor our parents in their old age (Exodus 20 v 12).

This should be our expectation, not an exception. But sadly, as a pastor I've often seen Christian children show little regard for elderly parents. At times I've had to literally beg adult children to visit the bedside of their aging parent, to come and help make critical decisions.

Caring for the elderly isn't an option for us. It's a requirement. The Bible has a strong word for those who neglect aging family members: you are worse than an unbeliever (1 Timothy 5 v 8). We follow a Lord who, as he hung on the cross, bleeding and dying, made sure his mother, Mary, would be cared for after he left the earth (John 19 v 25-27).

To care for those in their final stages of life is to recognize their dignity. It is to say that while their bodies or minds are failing, they are no less people, with no less dignity. It is to see what Paul sees in 2 Corinthians 4—a full person, though the body is fragile and broken—awaiting full redemption, and inwardly being renewed.

Of course, care-giving can often be repetitive, inglorious, and wearying, requiring difficult and complex choices about the end of life. This is where Christian communities must come alongside those who care for their elderly loved ones, providing respite and encouragement during these difficult seasons of life. The aging give those of us who are younger the opportunity to serve, which is part of the way we live out our mission as the people of God. It is a beautiful cycle of life: we are dependent on our parents as children and they are dependent on us at the end of their lives. We are to value care-giving as care-givers value those who need caring for. They say it takes a village to raise a child. And it takes a church to care for our elderly.

But we need to look beyond our own. Not too far from where you live, there will be many abandoned and lonely residents of nursing homes and assisted-living facilities. A high percentage rarely have visitors. Simply spending time at a nursing home is a simple way to show the love of Christ and give dignity to elderly persons. A friend of mine took some teenagers from his church to residential homes each Easter, to give out gifts and to share a little of the Easter message. At one, an elderly lady sobbed. A teenage girl put her arm round her and spoke with her. It turned out she received very few visitors, very rarely. And it transpired that she was herself a Christian—and had thought, as she sat for years in her home, that there were no young Christians anymore. That simple visit told her that she had dignity. That she was worth something. And that Christ was still building his church.

Visiting the elderly will not be glamorous. It may not be exciting for you. But it may be the most significant thing you do in your day.

ILLNESS AND THE KINGDOM OF GOD

The Christian vision of death and dignity should also inform the way we think about our bodies and our health.

Illness is part of the curse of the fall, and the healing of disease is a blessing of God's kingdom, glimpsed in Christ's first coming, and arriving in full when he returns. When answering the disciples of John who wondered whether or not he was the true Messiah, Jesus urged them to look at his miracles of healing as proof of his deity: "The blind receive their sight and the lame walk, lepers are cleansed and the deaf hear, and the dead are raised up" (Matthew 11 v 5). His new creation will contain no more pain (Revelation 21 v 4).

But what of the sickness and pain we endure while living between his first and second comings? It is right and good to pray for divine healing. The Bible tells us to pray with faith (James 5 v 14-15), knowing the Great Physician is able to heal.

However, we should also seek remedy through medical care. Paul urged Timothy to find relief for a stomach ailment (1 Timothy 5 v 23). These two approaches are not in contradiction. Jesus, after all, urged us to watch and pray. Seeking medical relief and prayer for healing work together. Sometimes our prayers simply bring us close to cures or a more accurate diagnosis or the means to secure treatment. Other times prayer may be met by healing. And there are times when God asks his servants to endure pain or suffering that will neither be healed in this life nor treated by medicine.

A message that God always heals in response to the right level of faith is a distorted gospel. It is a lie. Jesus himself promised tribulation and suffering (John 16 v 33). Some of Jesus' most devoted followers were called to suffer greatly before their deaths. The apostle Paul, for instance, asked three times for a specific physical burden to be lifted and three times God resisted Paul's entreaties (2 Corinthians 12 v 8). Did Paul not have enough faith? The Bible teaches the opposite of the so-called prosperity gospel. Yes, sometimes God does heal, even today, and we can ask him to do this for us and for our loved ones. But often God asks his most devoted servants to suffer excruciating physical maladies, and we must never demand that he heal.

Perhaps the most poignant contemporary example of faith in the midst of suffering is Joni Eareckson Tada, paralyzed over fifty years ago in a tragic diving accident. Joni, a quadriplegic confined to a wheelchair and without use of her limbs, has nevertheless been a faithful public witness for Christ. Her ministry, Joni and Friends, speaks out on behalf of the disabled and distributes free wheelchairs around the world. Joni has taught the church about what suffering with Christ looks like in ways that few of us will experience. In an interview, she recently talked about her difficult struggle with pain:

> *"For more than ten years I have dealt with chronic pain (very unusual for a quadriplegic like me). Piled on top of my quadriplegia, at times it seemed too much to bear. So I went back and re-examined my original views on divine healing to see what more I could learn. What I discovered was that God still reserves the right to heal or not to heal as he sees fit.*
>
> *"And rather than try to frantically escape the pain, I re-learned the timeless lesson of allowing my suffering to push me deeper into the arms of Jesus. I like to think of my pain as a sheepdog that keeps snapping at my heels to drive me down the road to Calvary, where, otherwise, I would not be naturally inclined to go."* [65]

Joni is a prime candidate for the "death with dignity" movement. Instead, she trusts God's goodness to help her endure her pain and struggling. If anyone would "qualify"

---

65 "A Purpose in the Pain: An Interview with Joni Eareckson Tada," Ligonier Ministries, accessed 11.18.17, http://www.ligonier.org/learn/articles/a-purpose-in-the-pain-an-interview-with-joni-eareckson-tada/.

to be healed of her maladies based on her faith, it would be Joni; yet she understands that God has worked through her ongoing pain, to draw her closer to her Savior and give her a public platform to proclaim Christ. She refuses to be defined by her pain or her disability. She finds her identity in being made by God and saved in Christ, and finds her purpose in serving him.

This is a life with dignity. It leads to a death with true dignity, and then a life on into eternity in the presence of our Maker.

Dignity in life, and dignity in death, are not found in avoiding suffering but in knowing Christ. Both the fake gospel that promises a life without suffering and the "death with dignity" movement that offers a death without pain are peddling false promises. Jesus offers something far more: knowledge of our unalterable value even in our darkest moments, and eternal healing in the place beyond pain and tears. In a sense, even the healthiest among us are in a process of dying, but, if we are in Christ, we are also in the process of being renewed. This hope is why Joni and millions of other Christ-following sufferers around the world can hang on. They can see, on the distant shore, their final healing to come.

THE HEALTH-CARE QUESTION

Human dignity also means we need to think carefully about health care. In the United States at least, this topic is extremely divisive, with the parties lined up on both sides blaming each other for the seemingly intractable problems with health care. But while Christians may differ on the best delivery system, we should agree that access to affordable care is an issue of human dignity.

Since the kingdom of God means that the lame will walk again and the sick will see their diseases healed, we image the kingdom of God by working for better solutions to get relief and cures to those who suffer from illness and disease. Our approach can't be to simply ignore the plight of the working poor whose lack of resources keep them from accessing quality health care and medicine. I'm particularly sobered by the way the prophets often speak against the indifference of those with means toward the vulnerable in their midst. Here is just one example:

> The LORD will enter into judgment with the elders and princes of his people; "It is you who have devoured the vineyard, the spoil of the poor is in your houses. What do you mean by crushing my people, by grinding the face of the poor?" declares the LORD GOD of hosts.

ISAIAH 3 V 14-15

Most of us are not health-care-policy experts. These are complex issues. But can we resolve not to settle for a society where there is enough wealth to give all people access to a good standard of health care, but in which we allow or acquiesce in maintaining a system where the faces of the poor are ground down in the moments of their greatest vulnerabilities?

Katelyn Beaty, former editor of *Christianity Today* and a pro-life champion, urges pro-life politicians to consider "enacting programs and policies that make it easier for millions of women to choose life, from pre- and postnatal care to delivery to high-quality child care and education and beyond."[66]

To not have health care in a wealthy country is to have dignity assaulted. Our neighbor's ability to find life-saving care should matter to us. If God has created us as humans,

---

66 "I'm a Pro-Life Evangelical. Republicans Are Pushing a Heath Care Bill That Isn't.," Vox, May 25, 2017, accessed 1.16.18, https://www.vox.com/first-person/2017/5/25/15659512/abortion-pro-life-ahca-republicans.

body and soul, then God cares about our bodies and the bodies of our neighbors.

This is, of course, not exclusively a government issue. I've been encouraged by the growing sense among evangelicals of the way that the church can step into some of these gaps and help provide care, especially in under-served areas. I've had the opportunity to tour some amazing church-funded clinics in both urban and rural areas. I've seen Christian doctors and nurses sacrifice time and money to use their gifts to serve in amazing ways.

The church cannot be the sole provider or even main provider of health care in most societies—there is an important role for governments to ensure the welfare of its citizens—but we can do much. Those of us with financial means might look for ways to help those without them, whether it's through the giving of our money to ministries that serve the medical needs of the poor or by advocating for policies that ensure their access to quality care.

And we can serve a powerful role in caring for the sick within our own congregations. As we serve each other by making meals, visiting, or paying for expenses, we show the world what it means to be God's people. Close-knit Christian community can help those struggling with hardships, whether it's terminal illness, debilitating chronic pain, or addiction. By our love we show the world what it means not only to be a Christian, but what it means to be human.

TOWARD THE CITY WITHOUT PAIN

A robust vision for human dignity and a clear view of our future hope help us live well now and care for those whose dignity is being assaulted. They frame the way we think about our bodies, about life, and about death.

Every time I make a visit to an elderly person who has nothing to offer me but their wisdom, every time I consider pain in my life as a trial transforming me into the image of Christ, every time I consider poor people's access to good-quality health care as I make voting decisions or pay my taxes, every time I draw alongside someone struggling with chronic pain or addiction and simply say, by my quiet presence, "I'm here for you," I am remembering and proclaiming that dignity is not earned by any creature; it is given by our Creator. And I am pressing the good news of dignity and resurrection into the broken places of the world and pointing people toward a city without pain, where the shadows of death will cease and we will finally be whole, body and soul. Let that be our story, lived and spoken.

8. GOOD WORK
WORK AND POVERTY

*"Every faithful act of service, every honest labor to make
the world a better place, which seemed to have been forever
lost and forgotten in the rubble of history, will be seen on
that day [at the final resurrection] to have contributed to
the perfect fellowship of God's kingdom."*

AMY SHERMAN

While my friends spent their Christmas breaks relaxing
or watching television or spending time with my other friends, I was forced to wake up at an obscenely early
hour, put on several layers of warm clothing, and will myself out into the world.

My father, for reasons that were a mystery to me in
my teenage years, thought it important for me to work
with him in his plumbing business. I worked with Dad on
almost every school break and most summers, installing
copper water lines, plastic drainage piping, and steel gas
lines in new homes. Though I knew early on that, unlike
Dad, I was not especially gifted to work in construction,
I got pretty good at plumbing houses. But more important than the opportunity to earn money (Dad paid well)
was the lessons I learned about hard work and Christian

calling. These lessons didn't really occur to me until well after I stopped working for my father and began to find my way in my own career.

Dad is not a trained theologian. He doesn't have a college degree. But he spoke into my life powerful lessons about the dignity of working hard and working well. Dad, a quiet man, is known to be a Christian by the quality of his work and the integrity of his character. I stopped counting the days when he insisted we stay on the job longer than I thought we needed to, simply so he could perfect his work. "But Dad," I learned not to bother to argue, "nobody will see those pipes in the wall. Why do you care about them being so straight and uniform?"

"Son," Dad would say, "I see it. And, more importantly, God sees it."

THE GIFT OF WORK

What I learned at Dad's knee is a vital part of what it means to be human. Work is good. This should not surprise us, since we are made in the image of a working God: "On the seventh day God finished his work" (Genesis 2 v 2). Jesus told the Pharisees that "My father is always at his work to this very day, and I, too, am working" (John 5 v 17, NIV).

Work, then, is a God-imaging gift that the Creator gives to his image-bearers:

> *When no bush of the field was yet in the land and no small plant of the field had yet sprung up—for the LORD God had not caused it to rain on the land, and there was no man to work the ground...* GENESIS 2 V 5

God's creative project is, in a real sense, incomplete without people, made in his image, working, cultivating, and stewarding his creation. It's almost as if Moses is making sure his readers understand that the cosmos will not work—cannot work—without humans cultivating it.

We are not made to worship the earth nor to exploit it. Image-bearers should be environmentalists in the best sense. We care about the earth because God created it for us to cultivate. And our work is not merely a by-product of life in the world—a necessary means to an end. Work is woven into our humanity. We were made to master the earth: to innovate and explore.

We image God by working hard in the world and by taking care of the world.

But of course, as with all of God's good gifts, our work is corrupted by the fall. Listen to the words of God as he speaks to Adam after his and Eve's sin:

> *Cursed is the ground because of you; in pain you shall eat of it all the days of your life; thorns and thistles it shall bring forth for you; and you shall eat the plants of the field. By the sweat of your face you shall eat bread…*
> GENESIS 3 V 17-19

The planet, once created in perfect harmony to be worked and tilled for God's glory, now groans in corruption (Romans 8 v 22), feeling the aches of the curse. The ground fights back. Work becomes hard and exhausting and, at times, a cycle of fruitless drudgery. Work, eat, sleep, work, eat, sleep. Then we die.

We are right to want our work to be fulfilling. We are wrong to think our work will never be free of being frustrating. In a created-yet-fallen world, we'll experience both fulfillment and frustration in our work.

Moreover, the gospel gives renewed purpose to our work. This doesn't necessarily mean that Christians are the best artists and craftsmen and administrators and stay-at-home moms and lawyers, but that the gospel helps us see the creative value of our work and points us toward the kingdom of God, where our labors will finally be free of the fall's thistles and thorns that steal our dignity. In Christ, God restores us to our original, image-bearing purposes:

> *For we are his workmanship, created in Christ Jesus for good works, which God prepared beforehand, that we should walk in them.* EPHESIANS 2 V 10

We do not work to be saved. But being saved, there is good work for us to do.

WORK IS NOT YOUR EVERYTHING

Because we live in a Genesis-3 world, we are tempted to think wrongly about our work, in two ways.

First, we can make our work everything: an object of worship and devotion instead of the good gift God created it to be.

Our careers are often seen as a marker of identity and worth. Consider the way a conversation goes when you meet someone for the first time. Next time you greet a visitor at church or strike up conversation on the train or meet a new family in your neighborhood, you will likely, without even thinking, ask, "So, what do you do for a living?" Their answer will, to some extent, inform the way you think of them.

I spend much of my time in either Nashville or Washington, D.C.—two cities where this question takes on heightened significance. In Nashville, a city blessed with a vibrant artist community, people are often defined by their creative acts. *I'm a songwriter. I'm working on a project with so-and-so. I'm working in marketing for this or that label/company/nonprofit.* In D.C., it's a power game, where business cards are exchanged and contacts are stored to leverage influence. *I work on the Hill on Ways and Means. I just started at this think tank. I work at this government agency.*

Think about the questions work often provokes:

- Is my job significant?
- Does it give me influence?
- Do people know what I do and do they think it matters?

We don't ask these questions out loud, of course, but we think them, subconsciously.

And so it is very easy to end up worshiping work as that which gives us our significance, our ultimate fulfillment. Sometimes it's important for us to step back and see what work, when worshiped as an idol, demands of us. We don't just leave it at the office or the factory floor—we take it home. It is in our pocket, always pulling us away from our family and friends with one more check of our email, one more phone call, one more quick project. Work whispers in our ears that we are God-like, without a need for rest.

If we are not careful, we will load our vocations with the weight of a significance they were not meant to bear. As long as we are working, productive, and influential, we think we are happy. We often don't even realize we've worshiped this faceless god until we've looked up and seen all of the unnecessary sacrifices we've made to it.

Work matters, and it matters to God, but it makes a poor god. We were not created in the image of our salaries or our positions or the organization for which we work. These good things will one day pass away, leaving us, if we are not careful, empty and unfulfilled.

This is why we must return, again and again, to the truth that our identity is not dependent on our utility or our influence or our paycheck, but is grounded in the love God has for his image-bearers. And in Christ, we know we are not merely laborers for corporations, but co-heirs with him forever. Tim Keller says that "faith gives you an inner ballast without which work could destroy you." [67]

WORK IS NEVER NOTHING

But then, second, we are also tempted to see our work as nothing.

I've heard variations of this sentiment in the churches I have served: "Pastor, I wish I could really serve Jesus like you do. I have to sling it in a factory or stuff bags on an airplane or serve coffee to college students."

This reflects an underdeveloped view of work, as if only what we do on Sundays when we meet as church "counts" as Christian service, and work is just the way we get a paycheck and the place we go to to try to evangelize.

Sadly, much of this exists because of misguided teaching and preaching. We pastors have often failed to teach a robust doctrine of work and have often elevated our own vocations higher on the heavenly org chart than God does. When we reduce the significance of our callings to mere utilitarian purposes, we diminish our own dignity. God did not create us as mere money-generating bots, but as creators, even if much of our creating seems mundane and monotonous.

Perhaps I'm particularly sensitive to this because I felt that vocations such as my father's were considered second-class by the church culture in which I grew up. It is too easy for those of us who receive paychecks from Christian organizations to consider our callings more sacred than those of the people we serve.

Constructive work is in and of itself a way we live as image-bearers. And the way we work can be a way we demonstrate

---

67 "Tim Keller: 5 Ways the Bible Shapes Our Work," Acton Institute PowerBlog, May 24, 2013, accessed 1.16.18, http://blog.acton.org/archives/55225-tim-keller-on-how-the-bible-shapes-the-way-we-work.html.

that we understand the value of those we work alongside, and those we interact with. Our work is how we love and serve our neighbors.

When my father gave full attention to installing plumbing systems that work, he was serving the family whose house he worked on, and thus the community and the world. A craftsman should make good products because fellow image-bearers will use them. A baker should produce delicious baked goods because they will be consumed by fellow image-bearers. A retail employee should stock shelves with excellence because those shelves will be perused by fellow image-bearers looking to purchase goods. And in all of this, our Father is watching, pleased with our honest labor (Colossians 3 v 23). Working with this perspective gives our work value, but never supreme value.

ARE YOU PHARAOH?

Work can enable us to flourish or it can cause our souls to shrivel. And the way we work will do the same for others, too.

Ambition blinds us to pursuing the good of those who work for us. So does laziness. All of us will be tempted to use our positions or our power to serve ourselves, which is always accompanied by the exploitation of others.

Exodus records an egregious example of exploitation. Pharaoh viewed the increasing Hebrew population with increasing suspicion and fear, as a threat to his power, so he weaponized work by exploiting the Hebrews for cheap labor:

> They set taskmasters over them to afflict them with heavy burdens. They built for Pharaoh store cities, Pithom and Raamses ... they ruthlessly made the people of Israel work as slaves... EXODUS 1 V 11-13

Rather than seek the Israelites' flourishing by using his power to create opportunities for them to live out their dignity by working, Pharaoh used his power to squeeze as much productivity out of the Israelites as he could. He refused to see their humanity; he considered only their utility. A slave class had economic benefits, so he made them work harder for longer hours and more wages. He ratcheted up the demands for productivity and scaled back natural rhythms of rest and refreshment. But God heard the cries of his people; he saw the injustice and exploitation, the dehumanization by grinding work. And he rescued Israel.

We might recoil in horror at Pharaoh's profiting from human capital in ancient Egypt, but we are still prone to use power as a means of exploiting those who might work with us or for us. A Christian vision of leadership should infuse the way we lead our organizations, our teams, or our ministries. I'm often amazed at the way Christian leaders, in the business world and in the non-profit world, poorly treat the employees who work for them, skirting labor laws, paying less than market wages, and demanding a work pace that is damaging to their employees' family lives. I've even heard leaders at Christian organizations brag, privately, at how good they are at firing people. Sometimes hard decisions like this have to be made, but they should be made with tears and not glee.

Those of us privileged to lead others, in any way, should constantly be asking: "Is my leadership contributing to their flourishing? Am I leading in a way that helps my team work hard, and well, and with integrity, without inviting them to make their work their god? Do I treat my fellow laborers as property or as people?"

This is important, not just for bosses but for workers at every level. Andy Crouch says that…

"in every workplace, Christians should be those who speak up most quickly, and sacrifice their own privileges most readily, for those whose image-bearing has been compromised by that

*organization's patterns of neglect. In every society, Christians
should be the most active in using their talents on behalf of
those the society considers marginal or unworthy."* [68]

Christians often balk at some of the work of labor movements. And to be sure, modern labor movements have
often overreached, hurting both worker and company. But
we should be among the most vocal voices urging for fair
wages, workplace safety, and adequate systems that allow
for rhythms of toil and rest. We need to see the humanity
of workers. Without protections, the powerful will always
be tempted to exploit the vulnerable.

It was God himself who put in place labor laws for
Israel when they moved out of Egypt and began living as
their own nation. The Sabbath was enforced as a weekly
rhythm of rest, not simply as a perk for the powerful but
for the entire country. It was the vulnerable—those who
live at the bottom rung of the ladder—who most needed
rest and likely had the least agency to practice it. God en-
sured Israel's leaders would obey his call to let everyone
cease their work, for work to be enjoyable and fruitful
once again, rather than exploitive. [69]

GOD CARES ABOUT POVERTY (AND SO SHOULD WE)

We cannot discuss work without looking at the tragedy of
poverty. Poverty is, at its root, created by conditions that
deny some people an opportunity to work for a fair wage.

The plight of the poor is a major theme in Scripture,
and one that faithful Christians cannot ignore. The prophets railed against the nations for their neglect of the

---

68 "The Three Callings of a Christian," accessed 11.11.17, http://andy-crouch.
com/extras/the_three_callings.
69 I originally heard this from a terrific sermon on Exodus 31 by Matt Chandler,
"Work and Rest," The Village Church, April 9, 2017, accessed 1.16.18, http://
www.tvcresources.net/resource-library/sermons/work-and-rest.

poor. The Psalms cry out with the poor's desperation and God's promise to hear them. And, most importantly, the in-breaking of Jesus' kingdom is seen as "good news for the poor" (Luke 4 v 18), in a fulfillment of Isaiah's prophecy (Isaiah 61 v 1).

God cares about the poor because poverty—the lack of basic decent human needs—is an assault on the dignity of people. Grinding poverty dehumanizes both physically and spiritually. Christians ought to care about the poor, not simply or primarily because it makes us feel good or because fighting poverty makes the world look kindly on us but because caring for the poor is intrinsic to a holistic gospel message.

If the kingdom of God is indeed good news for the poor, then Christians—particularly Christians who live in wealthy nations—have a moral responsibility to both give generously to help alleviate human suffering and to work hard to change systems that perpetuate poverty. Loving our neighbors as ourselves means seeking their flourishing. The apostle John warns against indifference to the poor:

> *But if anyone has the world's goods and sees his brother in*
> *need, yet closes his heart against him, how does God's love*
> *abide in him?* 1 JOHN 3 V 17

Helping the poor begins first by seeing them. We are often trained to turn our eyes away from those who are less fortunate, because they make us feel uncomfortable and this reality may call us to a kind of sacrifice we are not willing to make.

But by seeing the poor, we see their humanity, and thus their dignity—and we allow ourselves to be challenged and moved to bear a cost to make a difference.

The church, at its best, has recognized poverty-alleviation as part of its mission. Historian Kyle Harper writes of the early church's application of the image of God to the poor:

"The worth of the poor was inherent in their humanity. The high rank of the poor was assured by the fact that God had lent them his own personhood. The respect due to the poor by virtue of their humanity was imperiled by the very experience of poverty and disease." [70]

This is what motivated my friend Rich Stearns to leave his comfortable life as the CEO of a luxury goods company nearly twenty years ago and lead the humanitarian relief agency World Vision. World Vision is the largest Christian relief organization in the world, bringing help and hope to the most broken places in the world. World Vision brings clean water, education, medical care, and other vital resources to desperate places in the world. They care for refugees in crisis and help under-resourced communities develop economically.

Stearns told me that what motivates him is...

"to combine the Great Commandment and the Great Commission. So the Great Commission is to go into all the nations and make disciples for Christ and the Great Commandment is about loving our neighbors as ourselves ... when you love people and you care about their physical situation, you earn the right to speak into their lives about what motivates you and the answer is the Gospel. It is the Good News of Jesus Christ that God did so much for me that I care about you." [71]

Organizations like World Vision, Baptist Global Response, Compassion International, International Justice Mission and a thousand other Christian humanitarian organizations leverage the time, resources, and money from Christians

---

70 Shah and Hertzke, *Christianity and Freedom: Volume 1*, page 140.
71 "The Way Home Featuring Rich Stearns," accessed 11.11.17, www.danieldarling. com/2017/03/the-way-home-featuring-rich-stearns/.

around the world to meet human need. They say, *The poor exist. They are human. They matter to God and so they must matter to us.*

Not all of us are called to do what Rich Stearns did and lead humanitarian organizations. But all of us are called to sacrifice something for the flourishing of others.

BEYOND CONSERVATIVE AND LIBERAL APPROACHES

In countries where we have a say in the kind of government that leads us, poverty should be a consideration— and a major one—when we decide who will get our vote.

But this is where it gets tricky and complicated. On the one side, liberals believe strongly in the power of the state to alleviate human suffering. On the other side, conservatives believe strongly in the power of the free market and private social institutions, particularly the church, to alleviate suffering.

How should Christians think through this? How does the language of human image-bearing dignity help us?

First, though I'm not a liberal in the political sense, I am grateful that liberals refuse to let us forget the plight of people who are poor, especially those who are poor in our own prosperous countries. While many of us live comfortable lives, there are many, even within walking distance of our homes, who do not know where they will sleep tonight or what they will eat. Those who push for state solutions to inequality and poverty are right to remind us that the poor are a collective concern. From Scripture we learn that God judges nations by the way they treat people who are poor (Amos 2 v 7; Ezekiel 16 v 49). God seems to hold nations—and by extension those who make voting and policy decisions in nations—accountable. We will be judged by God for the way we leveraged our power.

At the same time, we should be wary of increasing the size and scope of the state and, more importantly, the way that government programs often work against the dignity of those they are trying to help. Liberals would be wise to note the ways the state might deliver aid in often inefficient and costly ways. Well-meaning government programs can, at times, work against raising of people out of poverty. If we genuinely care for those who are poor, we should seek to recognize their dignity by finding ways to invest in communities for long-term recovery, and ways in which they can fully live out their image-bearing purposes by working and creating and helping their neighbors flourish.

Chris Horst and Peter Greer, whose organization Hope International works to create viable businesses in developing countries through micro-loans, say, "Entrepreneurship creates the opportunities for people to experience what it means to be truly human."[72] Even the singer Bono, no raging capitalist, has acknowledged the importance of systems that lift people from dependence to entrepreneurship.[73] This is why our charity, both private and governmental, must see the whole person and work to ensure their dignity by the agency of work.

At the same time, just as liberals should not have blind faith in the power of the state to alleviate human suffering, conservatives like me should be wary of blind faith in the free market and private institutions, even the church, to alleviate suffering. Markets, at their best, leverage human incentive and ingenuity for the flourishing of society. Markets

---

72 Peter Greer and Christ Horst, *Entrepreneurship for Human Flourishing* (Aei Press, 2014), page 74.

73 "U2's Bono Courageously Embraces Capitalism," Forbes, accessed 6.14.17, http://www.forbes.com/sites/markhendrickson/2013/11/08/u2s-bono-courageously-embraces-capitalism/.

reward hard work and thrift. But capitalism, while a good system, can be a deeply flawed system as well. It can often incentivize greed and leave many behind. It does nothing to prevent the rich exploiting the poor or to restrain corporations from treating their employees like mere figures on a balance sheet. There are many good things about capitalism, but we should be wise to its drawbacks.

Conservatives sometimes point out that if the church were doing its job, we wouldn't need government poverty programs. And Christians in wealthy countries could do much more than they are. One survey estimates that American Christians, for instance, only give away 2.5% of their income.[74] Imagine if that average were at 10%, the standard that some use for giving their tithe. One estimate says this would generate $165 billion dollars in additional money that could be used to help the world's most vulnerable. This lack of generosity on the part of Christians in the world's wealthiest country is not just a problem; it's a scandal. But even $165 billion would not and could not cover the scope of human need in our communities. And in some nations, the Christian footprint is far smaller, and thus fewer resources are available to, and therefore through, churches. There has to be a role for the government to provide some kind of safety net—some assistance for those who find themselves without resource and agency.

So rather than assuming our prior political or economic position is correct, here is what we should be asking: "What is the most efficient delivery system for care for those in need? What policies help sustain lasting flourishing? How can the church, the market and the state work together to lift people from hope to despair?"

---

74 "What Would Happen If the Church Tithed?," *RELEVANT Magazine*, March 8, 2016, accessed 1.16.18, https://relevantmagazine.com/god/church/what-would-happen-if-church-tithed.

We also need to be wary of the way we are tempted to patronize those who are poor while seeming to advocate for their welfare. People who struggle financially are real, whole human persons, not props for photo ops. They are not vehicles through which to display our own self-righteousness or to score cheap points against political opponents. Even the phrase "the poor" (which I've aimed to avoid using in this chapter) is often unhelpfully depersonalizing.

We need a compassion that truly helps. Sometimes our charity reeks of condescension, and we use the poor as a way of signaling our virtue. Sometimes our compassion is also unhelpful and unintentionally suppresses local economies. If we are rightly pressing in on the call to live generously and open-handedly, we should do our homework before we invest and ensure that our resources can be best leveraged for the most human good.

DO SOMETHING

The scope of the world's need can be overwhelming, to be sure. So how as ordinary Christians can we follow Christ and use our gifts and resources to come alongside those who are suffering economically?

We might begin by spending intentional time in prayer, asking God to make clear where he is leading us, repenting of ways we've ignored the vulnerable, and asking him to make clear where he would like us to serve him in his mission in the world. Our work for the kingdom is not about us changing the world, but about joining what God is already doing in the world.

We would also be wise to do our homework and invest in institutions already doing good and effective work. For instance, a few years ago, *Christianity Today* studied the effectiveness of child sponsorships in bringing lasting, sustained relief to impoverished communities.[75] This motivated our family to begin investing in child sponsorships through Compassion International. Other ministries, like World Vision and Hope International see the value of micro-loans that help communities establish their own economic profit systems. This is just one, of many examples, of organizations already established who are ready for us to come alongside and meet human need.

Of course, the most important organization in the world is the one Jesus initiated by his life, death, resurrection, and sending of the Spirit. The church of Jesus Christ, though flawed, is the only institution guaranteed to exist forever. Jesus said that he would build the church and the "gates of hell would not prevail against it" (Matthew 16 v 17-19). We need to be careful, in our zeal to do something, of embarking upon an exhausting, lone-ranger, save-the-world activism. The Great Commission and Great Commandment were not given to a person, but a people. By working primarily (but not exclusively) through the institution created by God to reflect his glory, the body of Christ, we combine and use our unique gifts to care for others both around the corner and around the world.

Just today, as I type this, I'm marveling at the way my simple tithe money reverberates in mission throughout the world. It goes to a network of missionaries around the world who combine gospel proclamation and economic development in coming alongside the vulnerable. It helps pay for the third-largest disaster-relief operation in the world. It goes to local efforts in our city to help people flourish through homeless ministry, refugee work, and efforts to improve our local schools. Giving sacrificially through our

---

75 Bruce Wydick, "Want to Change the World? Sponsor a Child," Christianity Today.com, accessed 11.11.17, http://www.christianitytoday.com/ct/2013/june/want-to-change-world-sponsor-child.html.

local churches is far from the only way to combat inequality and poverty in our communities and in the world, but, in my view, it is the best place to start. There is no Christian who truly cares about poverty who does not give sacrificially through their church. And then from there we can work outward and endeavor to come alongside institutions, both local and national, who are doing effective work.

And sometimes, the way we recognize the dignity of people who are poor will not be as grandiose as launching a non-profit or traveling across the ocean, but will be the simple, everyday action of stopping to befriend a homeless man or volunteering at a local shelter. It could be as simple as giving a person in need a job or tutoring a child with special needs.

When we perform these small acts, whether close to home or around the world, we are imaging the kingdom of God. In this life, we'll never fully experience the dignity of work as God intended in the Garden of Eden, and we'll never fully fill the pockets of despair that create grinding poverty. But we can have a renewed vision for our work— one that reflects our image-bearing purposes and that points others to the day we all long for, when both rich and poor find true flourishing in the new Jerusalem. Until that day, never let the fact that you cannot do everything mean that you do not do something.

9. THE BETTER STORY
IDENTITY, SEXUALITY, AND MARRIAGE

"How much larger your life would be if your self could become smaller in it ... You would break out of this tiny and tawdry theater in which your own little plot is always played, and you would find yourself under a freer sky, in a street full of splendid strangers."

G.K. CHESTERTON

There is a close connection between the way we see ourselves and the way we see the world. At the root of our fallenness is a tendency to turn inward, away from the God who created us. Sandra Richter calls this the "crime of the garden." God asked Adam and Eve...

"'Are you in? Do you want this? The only requirement is that I stay God, and you stay image. I'm the original; you're the copy. My very character defines what is good and evil, and you submit to those boundaries.' And Adam and Eve said no. They said basically, 'We want to create God in our own image. We do not want God creating us in his.' That's the crime of the garden."[76]

---

76 Q&A with Dr. Sandra Richter, "The Servant, the Idol, & the Image of God: Isaiah's Conversation with the Creation Account," Henry Center for Theological Understanding, February 8, 2017, accessed 1.16.18, http://bit.ly/2EP83sV.

Self-worship was the seduction offered in Eden. The first humans decided that it wasn't enough to represent God in the world. In acquiescing to the plans of the serpent, they sought to be gods over the world—to supplant God:

> *Although they knew God, they did not honor him as God or give thanks to him, but they became futile in their thinking, and their foolish hearts were darkened. Claiming to be wise, they became fools, and exchanged the glory of the immortal God for images resembling mortal man and birds and animals and creeping things.* ROMANS 1 V 21-23

The world is broken because humanity has rejected God's rule and worshiped false gods. This is why idolatry is given so much attention in the Old Testament. After God renewed his covenant with Noah in Genesis 9 and reiterated his love for humanity by reminding Noah and his family of their status as image-bearers, there is no more "image of God" language in the Old Testament—only warnings against idolatry. But in a sense, that is still "image of God" language, for in warning against idols, God was constantly warning his people that they could either worship their self-created images as gods or, as image-bearers, worship the One who created them.

Israel was to be the radical people of God, called to worship not gods of stone but the I AM, the God who had made everything and yet who could be known personally—the God who could not be seen or touched and whose mere shadow made Moses' face glow as he descended Mount Sinai after spending time in his presence (Exodus 34 v 29-35).

Idolatry is offensive to God because false deities represent a rejection of the purposes we were divinely created for. Idolatry is dust that was fashioned into God's likeness and given breath by God deciding to say to him,

"I don't need you and I don't want you." Instead of living as images of God, we fashion our own images in our own likenesses and expect them to do what only God can do. Domesticated deities don't represent creativity, but rather a failure of imagination, as we settle for a broken vision of paradise instead of the glorious end for which we were created. Worshiping idols dehumanizes us, by definition.

SEEING GOD IN THE MIRROR

Today, of course, there are still many people around the world who bow to false deities in physical temples. But in the West, the chief false god we worship is the one which looks back at us in the mirror. No religion is more ascendant in our secular societies than the worship of self. Columnist David Brooks describes this ethos well:

> *"We now live in a world in which commencement speakers tell students to trust themselves, listen to themselves, follow their passions, to glorify the Golden Figure inside. We now live in a culture of the Big Me, a culture of meritocracy where we promote ourselves and a social-media culture, where we broadcast highlight reels of our lives."* [77]

Our doing it "my way," to quote Frank Sinatra, always leads to disastrous results for the human race, including the member of it whom we see in the mirror. Our self-worship causes us to violate our brothers' and our sisters' dignity. It is what produces shame, and restlessness, and the nagging sense that what we pursued to give us what we need has in fact left us further from finding it. In trying to become God, we actually become less than human.

---

77 "When Cultures Shift," The New York Times, April 17, 2015, accessed 2.20.18, https://www.nytimes.com/2015/04/17/opinion/david-brooks-when-cultures-shift.html.

Self-worship leads to despair, because idolatry is a broken cistern, always taking and never satisfying (Jeremiah 2 v 13). The great tragedy of Western culture is that the image we have chosen to worship in place of God is the only one made in the image of God: us.

THE SOUNDTRACK OF OUR AGE

Self-love does two things: it both enslaves and causes us to objectify and dehumanize others.

There are many manifestations of self-love, but perhaps the most powerful is the sexual revolution. Its central belief statement of "If it feels good, do it" has become the soundtrack of our age. This is essentially an updated version of the serpent's original claim: that to live by our own truth is better than to submit to the truth of the Creator, who made and ordered the world.

God created men and women with differences and distinctions and called them beautiful. We have sought to reorder gender and sexuality in a way that we feel is good.

God initiated human sexuality between a man and a woman in total, lasting commitment through marriage, as a signpost to Christ's love for his church. We have reinvented marriage to fit our desires and priorities, and to last as long as it fulfills and satisfies us.

God intended for commitment to lead to lasting happiness. We have decided that happiness or its lack is the measure of our willingness to remain committed.

God gave humanity sexuality as a beautiful expression of love for a spouse and, most importantly, as a signpost of his love for his church. We have exploited it for personal gratification and enabled it to exploit others through pornography and sex trafficking.

We must be honest as Christians and acknowledge that the church has not always offered a positive, compelling vision for human sexuality. We've not presented the Bible's holistic and beautiful vision for sexuality, and we have often ended up only speaking of the negative consequences of sin in this area of life. We have, at times, emphasized the "not even a hint" warnings from Ephesians 5 v 3 without marveling at the beautiful mystery of sex within its intended place of marriage between one man and one woman, for which Ephesians 5 tells us to give thanks (v 4).

We have also, at times, provided little room for honest discussions about broken sexuality. We can do better at creating healthy spaces for people who are being tempted, or who have given in to temptations, to express their struggles and admit their failures and find help and support in community with others. We've been quick to point out the sin of homosexuality while winking and nodding at the heterosexual cohabitation happening among our young adults, or the glances (or worse) outside marriage occurring among our older adults. We've offered a less-than-compelling vision for the good calling of singleness (1 Corinthians 7 v 7), presenting it as a second-best status to be endured. We've pretended that the pornography epidemic isn't happening in our pews without recognizing its enslaving hold on so many who listen in shame without ever hearing of the grace that is available or the help we can (or should) be ready to give.

We have not spoken of and celebrated the beauty of sex as God created it to be enjoyed; and yet at the same time, we have often not acknowledged some of the ways in which sex is not always beautiful in this fallen world. Sometimes well-meaning churches have sent a message that marital intimacy is always "hot" and "the best kind of sex," when the reality is that sex is often difficult, including between committed spouses. And it is this void that has often left a vacuum filled by the false promises of the sexual revolution. For false is what those promises have proved to be: a movement that promised freedom has ended up creating a world where people are treated with less dignity.

Women are objectified in pornography. Children are left without fathers. The majority of marriages experience the pain of adultery. The hook-up culture has left many feeling hollowed out inside and without genuine intimacy and affection. Ironically, most sociologists agree that in an age of free love, people are more isolated, insecure, and alone than ever before.

Is that really the freedom we are looking for?

We need, in many ways, a recovery of the timeless and beautiful Christian vision for our beauty and our sexuality and our bodies. God's purposes for sexuality find their expression in the good complementarity of the committed, lifelong, sexually and emotionally faithful, male-female relationship God calls marriage. But why does God call this good? Why is this better? Why is this beautiful?

A TRUER BEAUTY

Moses, when narrating God's creative acts, makes a point of saying that in creating male and female, he created them both in his image (Genesis 1 v 26-27). Men, living out their distinctive purpose, image God in the world. And women, living out their distinctive purpose, image God in the world.

And God intended for men and women to come together in marriage to enjoy a relationship in which we can be naked and not ashamed (Genesis 2 v 25).

Marriage celebrates and showcases commitment and self-giving; and provides a place where we can be vulnerable and trust that we will be known and loved and supported— the kinds of experiences that humans instinctively long for, but seldom find. Marriage says to us, *Whatever happens, and however this goes, I will still be here tomorrow. The only thing that can part me from you is death.* Sex within marriage says, *I am passionately devoted to you, with all that I am.* This is the kind of relationship we all long for. Faithfulness is really what we seek for in all of our important relationships, in our communities, in our institutions. We need the kind of stability that guarantees that, unless and until death intervenes, fathers and mothers will sacrificially be present with and for their children.

And so marriage, as a lifelong, committed, faithful partnership between a man and a woman reflects God's ultimate mission in Christ's union with his own bride, the church. When Paul lays out how a husband is to love his wife and how a wife is to love her husband in this one-flesh relationship (Ephesians 5 v 31), he finishes by commenting that, "this mystery is profound, and I am saying that *it refers to Christ and the church*" (v 32, my italics). The intimate commitment of this lifelong union between a husband and wife is a celebration of the eternal intimacy between Christ and his people: of the passion with which Christ pursued us, and the passion that saw him come near to us, give himself for us, and bring us to himself as his beloved bride.

Christians are part of that bride. And so we are free to celebrate the wonder of sex and to celebrate far more the wonder that it points to: our union with Christ. We are free to make neither too much of sex (by treating it as everything); nor too little of sex (by viewing it as nothing at all—something to be thrown around outside marriage or to be treated as something to be strangely ashamed of within marriage).

But how is this good for those who are not married? Even those called to the good calling of singleness celebrate, by their faithful celibacy, what God has given to others by the gift of marriage. Their chastity is a homage to the purposes of sexuality and commitment between a married husband and wife. The single and celibate Christian is showing that the powerful urges of our sexuality—whether enjoyed within marriage or controlled without—are but temporary signposts, pointing to the intimacy of relationship with Christ as part of his people now and in eternity with him in glory. The good news for single people, as for married people, is that there is far more than sex. There is far more than human marriage—even than the perfect marriage that only the first man and woman have ever experienced. There is Christ, who makes us fully human.

THE DESIRE PROBLEM

For now, Christian or not, we live in a Genesis-3 world. Here, sin has disordered all our sexual desires. And the lie Satan whispers to us is that we are the sum total of our sexuality, and that we can and must therefore find our identity in our sexual desires. *This is just who you are. Be true to yourself. You'll only be yourself if you do what feels right. That's the way to be alive.*

But the truth is that nurturing fallen sexual desires, or any temptation for that matter, doesn't make us more fully human; it makes us less so. It doesn't point us to something more wonderful; it only turns us inward in unsatisfying self-worship. Someone always gets hurt. Someone always gets treated without dignity; even if it is "only" ourselves. Not all our desires are good. Not all our desires truly tell us what is best for us. Your disordered desires "wage war against your soul", the apostle Peter warns (1 Peter 2 v 11). Misdirected sexual fulfillment turns us away from transcendent wonder.

Increasingly, it's not just Christians casting doubt on the promise of the sexual revolution. Christine Emba, a columnist for the *Washington Post*, wonders if "we might pursue the theory that sex possibly has a deeper significance than just recreation." [78] Perhaps unrestrained desire is not good for our humanity.

These questions are why the Bible's vision of gender and sexuality is truly good and beautiful, and affirms our dignity—even when it asks us to live contrary to what we feel deeply we need in that moment. It communicates that sex is beautiful, but that we are much more than our sex lives. Our sexuality, whether we are single or married, can be a signpost to something beyond ourselves—to a deeper intimacy with Christ. The Creator's intent for his image-bearers ultimately helps humanity flourish. It is based on the idea of commitment and honor, and points to a greater glory in Christ's love for his church. It is an antidote for a world beset by sexual brokenness, exploitation, and heartbreak.

It is always far better to root our identity in being made by God and loved by God than to seek to make it ourselves and ground it in being loved by ourselves or another. Seeing ourselves in light of the God who made us and died for us tells us we are loved and valuable. This status doesn't change, unlike our feelings or our sense of ourselves. The Bible makes and proves the case that we are actually not designed to be deities. We are poor masters of our own fates. We are poor stewards of our own identities. We are poor objects of our worship. God is a better Father, a better Lord, a better King, a better God.

---

78 "Let's Rethink Sex," *Washington Post*, November 26, 2017, accessed 1.16.18, https://www.washingtonpost.com/opinions/lets-rethink-sex/2017/11/26/d8546a86-d2d5-11e7-b62d-d9345ced896d_story.html.

THE HEART OF YOUR IDENTITY

Jesus offers us rescue from the enslavement of our desires. Where the first Adam failed and plunged humanity into sin, the second Adam, Jesus, succeeded. Jesus, as the perfect image of God, accomplished what humanity cannot. Where the first Adam rejected his image-bearing status and pursued the cheap and false substitute god of "self," Jesus is the perfect image of God. Where Adam gave in to temptation, Jesus resisted temptation. Where Adam died for his own sin, Jesus was able to die for ours. And so he restores us to our original image-bearing purposes and conforms us into his image. By his Spirit, he keeps his promise to give his people a new heart, with new desires:

> *I will give you a new heart, and a new spirit I will put within you. And I will remove the heart of stone from your flesh and give you a heart of flesh. And I will put my Spirit within you, and cause you to walk in my statutes and be careful to obey my rules.*   EZEKIEL 36 V 26-27

Jesus invites us into the life we were originally designed to live. As God's recreated masterpieces (Ephesians 2 v 10), the gospel reorients us, recreates us, and restores us to that original image-bearing purpose. I love how the theologian Michael Horton envisions our new identity:

> *"Who am I? I am one who exists as a result of being spoken by God. Furthermore, I am one of God's covenant children whom he delivered out of ... sin, and death. I am one who has heard his command but not fulfilled it, one in whom faith has been born by the Spirit through the proclamation of the gospel. Because human beings are by nature created in covenant with God, self-identity itself depends on one's relation to God. It is not because I think, feel, experience, express, observe, or will, but because in*

*the totality of my existence I hear God's command and
promise that I recognize that I am, with my fellow image-
bearers, a real self who stands in relation to God and the
rest of creation."* [79]

You are not the sum total of your desires. You are not,
at the heart of your identity, gay or straight. You are not
single or married. You are not good or bad. You are God's
image-bearer. You are, through faith in Jesus, a reconciled
son or daughter of the King. You are, through faith in
him, a part of his bride.

HOW TO FIND YOURSELF

But although Christians are restored image-bearers, the
fight against self-love isn't as easy and glorious as it seems
when we are reading about it in a book like this. Even Paul
admitted the intensity of his daily struggle:

> *For I do not understand my own actions. For I do not do
> what I want, but I do the very thing I hate.*

> ROMANS 7 V 15

Being a new creation in Christ doesn't necessarily mean
our temptations go away. In fact, becoming a follower of
Jesus brings a new level of intensity, a renewed awareness of our own sin. This reminds us of who we are and
who we were. We "abstain from the passions of the flesh"
because we are "sojourners and exiles" (1 Peter 2 v 11).
This new life in Jesus calls us to something radically out
of step with some of our most passionately-felt instincts,
and out of step with many of our culture's most passion-
ately-preached norms. This is because Jesus calls us to live
not in self-love but in self-sacrifice:

---

79 *The Christian Faith: A Systematic Theology for Pilgrims on the Way* (Zondervan, 2011),
    page 405.

If anyone would come after me, let him deny himself and take up his cross and follow me. MATTHEW 16 V 24

This kind of self-denial doesn't always sound like good news, but we have to remember that the self we are denying is no longer our true self, but the fallen self. It does not feel like it, but we are denying the impulse to live in a way that dehumanizes us. When Jesus calls us to come and die, he is also inviting us to come and live. Here is the great paradox: it is in denying ourselves that we find ourselves, because it's in denying the temptation to worship ourselves, build our own identities, and bow down to our feelings that we are able to enjoy worshiping God, bow down to him, and live out our true identity as his image-bearers.

It will always be easier to recreate God in our own image, to suit our own desires, than to worship the God who made us in his image. As Robert George writes:

> *"Many believers ... are being led into a ... belief in an imaginary God made in the image and likeness of man. It is a most convenient 'God' who is always willing to say, 'Do whatever you feel like doing, darling; I love you just the way you are.'"* [80]

But this is not the Jesus we see in Scripture, whose presence is constantly disrupting and reordering our lives so he can remake them. All of us are called to come and die so that we can find the way to truly live. My friend and brother Sam Allberry, a pastor who experiences same-sex attraction, writes:

> *"Ever since I have been open about my own experiences with homosexuality, a number of Christians have said something*

---

80 "Victoria Beeching and Plato's Third Form of Atheism," *First Things*, accessed 8.4.17, https://www.firstthings.com/blogs/firstthoughts/2014/08/victoria-beeching-and-platos-third-form-of-atheism.

like this: 'The gospel must be harder for you than it is for me,' as though I have more to give up than they do. But the fact is that the gospel demands everything of all of us. If someone thinks the gospel has somehow slotted into their life quite easily, without causing any major adjustments to their lifestyle or aspirations, it is likely that they have not really started following Jesus at all." [81]

The real Jesus always disrupts our comfortable life and calls us to that life of cross-bearing. But the real Jesus can rescue us and change us. The real Jesus can bring us home to the place where we are able to enjoy being human, with only life-enhancing desires and without any sin to fight. The real Jesus gives us his Spirit to help us on the way there, and to lift us up when we fail. The real Jesus is present in our brokenness as we journey on toward perfection.

This is good news for those who are same-sex attracted. And this is good news for the many who struggle with gender dysphoria: with the feeling that the sex of their body is out of step with how they see themselves. There is a better story for this than the promises made by the transgender movement: that futile attempts to re-engineer biology will bring ultimate happiness. There is a better story than is sometimes offered by the church's distorted vision of a hyper-masculinity or hyper-femininity. Though few of us understand the pain and the torment of gender dysphoria, in a sense we can all identify with ways that we feel out of place in our earthly existence. Some struggle with anorexia, some struggle with body shame, some suffer from chronic pain or disease or dysfunction. All of us struggle against temptation. All of us have to weigh up competing voices about what it will mean to be really alive as human men or women. All of us will need to struggle, by the Spirit's

---

81 *Is God Anti-Gay?* (The Good Book Company, 2013), page 12.

help, to keep listening to the promise of the world God will restore us to. The Scripture says that our struggle is part of creation's groaning: the longing for final resurrection, restoration, and renewal (Romans 8 v 22-23).

I'm comforted by the way Paul addressed the ways in which our physical bodies seem to disappoint:

> *We are afflicted in every way, but not crushed; perplexed, but not driven to despair; persecuted, but not forsaken; struck down, but not destroyed; always carrying in the body the death of Jesus, so that the life of Jesus may also be manifested in our bodies.* 2 CORINTHIANS 4 V 8-10

This is a realistic description of life in a fallen world. Struggling. Wrestling. Confusion. Angst. Pain. But we can do this knowing that the end Jesus has in store for us is infinitely more glorious than any end we could imagine for ourselves:

> *So we do not lose heart. Though our outer self is wasting away, our inner self is being renewed day by day. For this light momentary affliction is preparing for us an eternal weight of glory beyond all comparison, as we look not to the things that are seen but to the things that are unseen. For the things that are seen are transient, but the things that are unseen are eternal.* 2 CORINTHIANS 4 V 16-18

We must believe that Jesus has a better story for our identity, for our bodies, for our lives than the one we create for ourselves. Until that final resurrection, we may never fully overcome the temptations that attack our souls, but we can cling to the hope of what is to come. Revelation describes the full reality of God's full, physical restoration at the end of the age, as we persevere in faith, where…

> *he will wipe away every tear from their eyes, and death shall be no more, neither shall there be mourning, nor*

crying, nor pain anymore, for the former things have passed away.　REVELATION 21 V 4

Our bodies, like our sex lives, are not nothing, but nor are they everything. We don't have to starve them, surgically alter them, or dress them up in such a way that we are slaves to cultural cues and our misleading desires. We can care for our bodies, and if and when possible enjoy our bodies, always remembering that we are more than our bodies—and that we are body and soul, redeemed by Christ, awaiting full redemption and final, liberating transformation.

HUGH HEFNER AND #METOO

Finding our own dignity in our identity as creatures of a loving Creator is the only way we can treat others with the dignity that God has given them. It is self-love that blinds us to the deep needs of the world around us, to the vulnerable. If I am busy being "true to myself," I can't offer myself in real, loving service to others. I won't serve others if I am only serving myself. I won't prioritize the dignity of others if I have made a god of my own desires. I won't deny myself to do what is best for others if my identity rests in being true to myself.

Perhaps the most vivid example of the way our self-love can keep us from respecting the dignity of others is that of Hugh Hefner, the founder of *Playboy*. When he passed away in 2017, the tributes to his supposedly liberated life flowed in. He was hailed as a champion who helped people leave their repressed sexual lives and embrace the revolution. But upon further scrutiny, the sad fruits of Hefner's life of self-love become plain. Ask the women who were paraded through the Playboy mansion. They'll tell you of the way they were objectified for Hefner's pleasure, and put before the world for the ogling and arousal of millions of men. What's more, Hefner's vision of sexuality helped usher in the era of pornography, which ensnares men (and women), destroys families, and contributes to the objectification of women (and men) around the world. Within a few months of those op-ed pieces praising Hefner's cause, Western culture was reckoning with the reality of sexual assault, as powerful men in Hollywood, the media, politics, sports, business, and even in the church were exposed as predators of women.

Our culture wants to say—rightly—that this kind of predatory behavior is not okay. Women are not objects for gratification, but whole persons, created in the image of God. Power should not be used to get what feels good. Self-love is not always the highest good. But of course, a culture that celebrates sexual liberation and brooks no compromise in the pursuit of doing what feels right has few grounds for restricting the pursuit of my desires in this way. It can only impose such restrictions by contradicting itself.

Christianity offers a better story. It says I am an image-bearer, under God's loving authority in whatever relational setting he gives, in the body he's given me. It says I've been "twice bought," in creation and redemption:

> *You are not your own, for you were bought with a price. So glorify God in your body.* 1 CORINTHIANS 6 V 19-20

This is a radical, counter-cultural way to look at the world. It seems like a paradox: when I think of myself less, I become more myself. When I unseat my desires from the throne of my heart, I'm more free.

Living free from the chains of desire allows us to more fully love our neighbor. We promote dignity in ourselves and others by living out God's purposes for our sexuality and our bodies. In doing so, we present those God-given bodies as living sacrifices (Romans 12 v 1), available to him and his mission. When we struggle on—when we say there are transcendent truths that are more important to our sense of self than what our culture has decided or what our desires are suggesting—we live out and we hold out the better story, in whatever place we've been given in it.

10. I AM NOT MY AVATAR
TECHNOLOGY AND OUR DIGITAL AGE

"It is easy ... to imagine that the next great division of the world will be between people who wish to live as creatures and people who wish to live as machines."

WENDELL BERRY

The world waits in hushed silence. Hundreds gather in the sleek new auditorium of the new multi-billion-dollar modern temple. Millions of others watch live on their smartphones, desktops, televisions, and even watches.

The date has sat unmoved on calendars while meetings, doctor's appointments, and deadlines get rescheduled. Media outlets spare no expense to cover the moment, deploying nervous journalists hunched over laptops, fingers nimble and ready to explain the moment to the world.

A leader ascends the stage, his body a slender figure against the massive image of his dead predecessor, the Founder, hologram-like on the wall behind him.

A deeply religious ritual, the spectacle draws a diverse audience of seekers: Fortune 500 CEOs and construction workers; busy executives and the people who tailor their shirts; soccer moms and urban hipsters. White collars, blue collars and no collars unite. They watch from the suburbs and they watch from the city. They watch in the West and they watch in the East. They watch everywhere.

Welcome to the annual secular sacrament known as the Apple Event (#appleevent).

And yes... I was one of those watching as Tim Cook climbed the steps of the stage at Steve Jobs' theater and preached the gospel of Apple, selling the world on the latest version of digital satisfaction. James Poniewozik of the *New York Times* describes the show this way: "People watch willingly, to get a glimpse of the new products and an art-directed idea of their better selves."[82]

Poniewozik is writing with tongue firmly in cheek, just as I have been so far in this chapter. But behind the satire is a truth about the way we approach our technology, and the way our technology approaches us. For, as Poniewozik says about his new iPhone:

> *"What will I do with it? What does anyone? I will Insta-gram photos of my cooking that I think look more ap-petizing than they are. I will see another tweet from the president. I will google song lyrics. I will read Facebook posts and get mad on the Internet.*
>
> *"And another year from now, I'll set another reminder to watch another Apple event, believing somewhere deep down that with one more upgrade, I might be perfected."*

Because that's the promise, isn't it? With the next upgrade, you'll be more the person you want to be. You'll be per-fected. That small black box in your pocket will remake and remold you into perfection.

---

82 "At the Apple Keynote, Selling Us a Better Vision of Ourselves," The New York Times, September 12, 2017, accessed 2.20.18, www.nytimes.com/2017/09/12/arts/television/apple-event-iphone.html.

CREATION CURMUDGEONS

Most of us have an ambivalent relationship with technology. We mock and yet watch #appleevent. We lament our enslavement to the glow of our smartphones as we read articles about said enslavement on our smartphones.

But rarely, if at all, do we ask: *what is a Christian to think about technology?*

To answer this complicated question, we need to begin with another: *what is technology, exactly?* When that word comes to mind, we typically think of modern stuff: smartphones and the internet and driverless cars. But is that really all technology is? After all, every generation has grappled with the disruption of new technologies, even before Apple (yes, there was a time before Apple). There was a time when objects we consider outdated or analog were on the cutting edge of innovation. Landline telephone, the railroad, and the printing press were all once the new technology.

Most of us, I think, operate on an assumption that technology is something we have to endure, but is not necessarily good—a kind of necessary evil. We feel a tad guilty and maybe a little grumpy, even as we argue that we need our devices to live in a modern world. We don't want to be Amish, rejecting virtually all technological innovations since eighteenth century—but we do wonder if maybe the Amish have a point.

But technology is simply the way in which image-bearers make things. And seen in this light, Scripture proves actually to be pro-technology. There are few people who have thought through this more than my friend Tony Reinke, author of *Twelve Ways Your Phone Is Changing You.* Tony describes technology as any...

"reordering of raw materials for human purposes ... the sweep of technological advance is a gracious gift from God to help us live in a fallen creation." [83]

Let's return again to that seminal passage on human dignity in Genesis and listen closely:

Then God said, "Let us make man in our image, after our likeness. And let them have dominion over the fish of the sea and over the birds of the heavens and over the livestock and over all the earth and over every creeping thing that creeps on the earth."

So God created man in his own image, in the image of God he created him; male and female he created them.

And God blessed them. And God said to them, "Be fruitful and multiply and fill the earth and subdue it, and have dominion over the fish of the sea and over the birds of the heavens and over every living thing that moves on the earth." And God said, "Behold, I have given you every plant yielding seed that is on the face of all the earth, and every tree with seed in its fruit. You shall have them for food. And to every beast of the earth and to every bird of the heavens and to everything that creeps on the earth, everything that has the breath of life, I have given every green plant for food." And it was so. And God saw everything that he had made, and behold, it was very good. And there was evening and there was morning, the sixth day.

GENESIS 1 V 26-31

Notice how Genesis describes God's ordering of creation. First, God creates humans in his image, and then he immediately delegates to humans the task of filling and subduing the earth. This is important. "Subdue" implies that God

---

83 *Twelve Ways Your Phone is Changing You* (Crossway, 2017), page 31.

intends for man to not leave his creation alone but instead to work it and form it and advance it. And that will require the application of what man finds in the world, coupled with his God-given creativity, to produce what he needs to subdue the world. It will require technology. This trait—the ability to create and innovate—is part of what makes humanity distinct from the rest of creation, and it is one important way in which we image God. There is dignity in creating technology. Technology is also not a thing outside of our humanity but an essential by-product of being human.

Technology is not merely a product of the twentieth and twenty-first centuries but has been with us since creation. We are not the first generation in human history to innovate and we most certainly will not be the last.

TECH BLESSINGS AND TECH CURSES

Technology blesses us.

I'm writing this chapter on a sleek computer with more processing power than the first space shuttle. I can easily look up Scripture via online software. I can access more theological works in the next two minutes than most of church leaders in human history had in their entire libraries. I drove to the coffee shop I'm working in today in a car, perfectly conditioned to the right temperature for my comfort. I'm sipping a beverage that arrived as a result of innovative new ways to filter and extract flavor from raw beans. I can text my thirteen-year-old daughter, who is babysitting our younger children, and give her instructions on how many minutes it takes to heat up their dinner in the microwave. My wife is currently attending a simulcast of a really good Bible teacher, beamed in from a church hundreds of miles away.

Not only that, but life-saving technologies are keeping people alive and healthy more than at any time in human history. My son has severe asthma. In previous eras, would he have had a chance at a normal life? Probably not. But today, due to innovation, he can be as active as any child.

But technology is a curse too.

The same internet that connects me to my family also provides a platform for terrorist groups to recruit and train new killers. The same air-travel technology that allows me to visit missionaries is also used to drop bombs on innocent civilians. The same screens that allow me to watch my favorite Bible teachers also beam soul-crushing pornography onto smartphones and tablets around the world, including into the rooms of children.

This is why, in order to think well about technology, we need both a Genesis-1 and Genesis-3 framework. The creative gifts given to us by our Creator can both serve God-glorifying, man-blessing purposes and, corrupted by sin, work toward evil ends. Technology can be the fruit of our mandate to subdue the earth or it can be a visible symbol of the way we are tempted to worship the creation more than the Creator (Romans 1 v 25). It connects and sustains while also dehumanizing and destroying.

So Christians need to both participate in the creation of new technologies and also ask critical questions about technology. We must continually ask ourselves not only what we are doing with technology but what technology is doing with us. Do the newest innovations promote dignity and enable us to express our image-bearing humanity? Or do they dehumanize us and rob us of our dignity?

MAKING THINGS TO WORSHIP

Writing around AD57, Paul described technology gone bad:

> *Claiming to be wise, they became fools, and exchanged the glory of the immortal God for images resembling mortal*

man and birds and animals and creeping things.

ROMANS 1 V 22-23

Don't miss the misuse of innovation and creation here. Humans, in their self-worship, made images—they applied their giftedness to create things—that they worshiped in order to reject living for God's glory. In a fallen world, technology can pull us toward misdirected loves and whisper lies about our identity that usurp our God-given role as image-bearers.

A month ago my iPhone suddenly was no longer able to receive a signal from my network provider, Verizon. This happened, as these things always do, during an extremely full season. It took about three to four frustrating days, several trips to the Apple Store, and phone calls (my desk phone at the office—how quaint) with Verizon before I was given a brand new iPhone. I quickly downloaded my information from the cloud and resumed my normal life.

What was revealing about these three to four days is how naked I felt. I felt unable to function, to manage, to live without my phone. And that was a revelation. My immersion in technology was telling me a lie about who I am and about who my Creator is. The author Trevin Wax describes this pathos: "The primary myth your phone tells you every day is that you are the center of the universe."[84]

Our devices give us the illusion of being all-powerful. Sick kid? I can look up the malady at midnight. Breaking news story? I can let the world know my opinion in a matter of seconds. Hankering for a hamburger? I can order one and have it delivered in minutes. My phone gives me the illusion that I am king of the world. When I'm sleepless or restless at night, I can reach over and grab my iPhone and plunge into new vistas of useless information, in an attempt to self-medicate by again finding a sense of control.

---

84 *This Is Our Time* (B&H, 2017), page 20.

We are often so immersed in our devices we fail to realize how much they diminish our humanity. But researchers are starting to pick up on this. In a recent essay for the *Wall Street Journal*, journalist Nicholas Carr cites several studies that show the pervasive influence of our smartphones, even when we are not actively engaging them. He writes: "Smartphones have become so entangled with our existence that, even when we're not peering or pawing at them, they tug at our attention, diverting precious cognitive resources. Just suppressing the desire to check our phone, which we do routinely and subconsciously throughout the day, can debilitate our thinking."[85]

Moreover, the flood of data that seems to make us more knowledgeable and more free of influence in fact makes us more dependent. One writer argues that, "Facebook would never put it this way, but algorithms are meant to erode free will, to relieve humans of the burden of choosing, to nudge them in the right direction."[86] The subsequent allegations about the way companies like Cambridge Analytica gather social-media-harvested data in order to influence opinions and even voting intentions gives credence to this view.

The truth is that many of us are, subconsciously, being shaped into the image of our own devices instead of being shaped into the likeness of Christ.

VIRTUOUS AND IMPORTANT?

Our devices also convince us that we are virtuous.

Think about the ways we broadcast our spirituality to the world: perfectly sunlit Bible, mug of coffee, rustic patio

85 "How Smartphones Hijack Our Minds," *Wall Street Journal*, October 6, 2017, accessed 1.16.18, https://www.wsj.com/articles/how-smartphones-hijack-our-minds-1507307811.

86 Franklin Foer, "Facebook's War on Free Will," *The Guardian*, September 19, 2017, accessed 1.16.18, http://www.theguardian.com/technology/2017/sep/19/facebooks-war-on-free-will.

table. Just think of the ways we project our families on Instagram or Facebook: neat and tidy, but not too serious, right? But have you ever thought about why we post the photos we do? Sometimes, of course, it is to send fun updates and pictures to our friends and family. But more often than not, I think, we are trying to make sure the world, or at least the world we want to impress, knows that we are good (through candid photos that probably took not an insignificant amount of time to stage!).

The temptation to project is especially pervasive in the way we do activism online. There is even a term for this: virtue-signaling. We want all the right people to know we are on the right side of the right issues. Virtue-signaling is, in many ways, a digital version of the story Luke tells of the Pharisee, in the temple, who loudly prays, to be heard among his peers: "God, I thank you that I am not like other men, extortioners, unjust, adulterers, or even like this tax collector" (Luke 18 v 11). *God, I thank you that I'm not like those other people who believe those things they are not supposed to believe.*

Ironically, virtue-signaling doesn't actually require any virtue. In some ways, we convince ourselves that online activity is a substitute for genuine activism. If we look as though we are doing something, we are doing something, right? This illusion of change is sometimes called slactivism.

And so our devices tell us that we are important.

The democratization of social media, so powerful when used for mobilizing movements opposing tyranny and as a vehicle for gospel proclamation, has also turned any person with a phone into a mini-celebrity.

This means that it is not only our view of ourselves that the latest technologies are changing. It is also our view of other humans. Arguing with an image on a screen instead of engaging in arguments face to face can dehumanize our opponents. People become avatars to be crushed. This is especially true when a public figure makes a public faux pas. The pile-on is quick and severe—part of what columnist David Brooks calls the "coliseum culture."[87]

Everyone is a journalist. Everyone is a public figure. Everyone has a platform. Have we ever stopped to ask ourselves: were we made for this? I'm especially nervous about the way in which social media has nurtured a kind of latent desire to be something or to tell ourselves we are something. I see this in the way it shortcuts paths to growth, for instance, in young seminarians or would-be activists.

There is a way that the illusion of influence bestows significance on us that we might find lacking in our offline lives. And the pressure to perform before a ready audience can nurture a subtle narcissism, where we live for public approval. I'll admit that I too regularly check my retweets. It's intoxicating. I need to ask myself: Dan, what does it profit you if you acquire hundreds of likes and lose your own soul?

But it's just so much easier to live online. Life is less complicated. My family always look good. I am always right. We are tempted to project a false self because we are, down deep, dissatisfied with our real selves. Reality is not virtual reality. It's messier. The real me has flesh-and-blood failings and is not as witty or wise, powerful or pithy as my avatar indicates.

The good news is that the gospel liberates us from our need to project a more airbrushed or corrected version of ourselves. Jesus doesn't ask me to present my best self to God, because God isn't impressed with my self-righteousness. He bids me come, just as I am. God's love isn't conditioned on the way we appear on the screen, but on his

---

87 "The Act of Rigorous Forgiving," *The New York Times*, February 10, 2015, accessed 1.13.18, https://www.nytimes.com/2015/02/10/opinion/david-brooks-the-act-of-rigorous-forgiving.html.

unconditional favor toward us in Christ. While we were yet sinners, Paul reminds us, Christ died for us. Jesus came to save sinners, not avatars. Clothed in his righteousness, I have nothing to prove. I can't hide from him behind my Facebook feed and Instagram images any more than Adam and Eve could hide from him behind trees in Eden. But I don't need to. I am freed to be myself.

Knowing we are made in God's image, and restored to relationship with him through Christ, means we can stop trying to fix ourselves via a projected goodness of virtue-signaling or carefully staged Instagram photos. The Spirit of God is already at work, sanctifying us, restoring the broken places, and transforming us into the image of Christ. We can rest in him, who knows and loves the real version of ourselves—the one we hide behind our digital fig leaves.

The significance we seek in the warm embrace of an expanded twitter following or a tidal wave of likes is a poor substitute for the affections of a heavenly Father. What is fifteen minutes of digital fame when compared to the glory of dining, one day, at the King's table?

SOME QUESTIONS

Uncritical engagement with technology can turn us away from worship of the Creator and toward worship of creation in ways that tell us lies about our humanity and drain away our dignity—which should leave us asking: what would it look like to wisely engage technology in a way that properly aligns our hearts and recovers our humanity?

I think it begins with us asking ourselves some simple questions, the answers to which we may not like:

• How is my use of technology separating me from the rest of my family and friends?

- Has my dependence on my devices replaced my dependence on God? In a moment of quiet, do I read my phone instead of praying to God?
- What quiet, physical aspects of my humanity is technology replacing?
- Do I need to separate myself physically from some forms of technology?

Most of us, if we are honest, have not stepped away from the glow of the screen long enough to wrestle with these questions. But we need to. One church I know of in London encourages a media fast for part of Lent each year—other than what's required for a member's work, there's no social media, no TV, no movies. Instead, they get together: to read Scripture, pray, or just hang out together. To many of us that will sound extreme—but perhaps our recoiling reveals something about us.

WELCOME TO THE iGEN
It's not just us, of course. It's our kids, too. I recently read a fascinating book by psychologist Jean Twenge, *iGen: Why Today's Super-Connected Kids Are Growing up Less Rebellious, More Tolerant, Less Happy—and Completely Unprepared for Adulthood—and What That Means for the Rest of Us*. Twenge studies the latest research on the behavior of the youngest generation, a generation she labels the "iGen"—the first generation to be fully immersed in a world of smartphones, social media, and cheap internet access.

In some ways, the findings are positive. By wide margins, iGen members are less likely to be afflicted with substance abuse, less likely to engage in reckless sexual activity, and less likely to commit violent crimes.

But… this generation is also more likely to suffer from depression and anxiety, and to admit to deep loneliness.

What seems to explain this is the massive shift in the way iGen interacts with other humans. Today's teens spend, on average, 6 to 8 hours a day in front of a screen, engaging some kind of digital media. They are less likely to hang out with friends (by an hour a week) than the previous generation of millennials; they attend movie theaters with less frequency; and they are less likely to drive. To put it bluntly, today's teens are more connected, but less social.

Again we see that technological innovation means some problems are lessened, and others are exacerbated (or even created). There is increasing isolation, pressure to perform, and stunted growth in developing social skills. There is a reason why tech-industry giants, who have pioneered these revolutionary devices, are limiting their usage in their own families. Melinda Gates, in a piece in the *Washington Post*, admitted her reluctance to allow her kids unfettered access to the screen. She says, "I spent my career at Microsoft trying to imagine what technology could do, and still I wasn't prepared for smartphones and social media." [88] Steve Jobs limited his own kids' device usage. [89]

As a parent of four iGen kids, this data has newly emboldened me to be intentional about the way I shepherd my kids into adulthood in this digital age. I'm more willing to be that weird parent that restricts my kids' screen time, to encourage them to read, and to cultivate environments where the full embodiment of their humanity can blossom in social situations. But as churches we need to think hard about how we might address the unique dehumanizing struggles—with loneliness, pressure to perform and

---

88 Melinda Gates, "I Spent My Career in Technology. I Wasn't Prepared for Its Effect on My Kids," *The Washington Post*, accessed 9.29.17, http://wapo.st/2ojYVW7.

89 "Steve Jobs Was a Low-Tech Parent," *The New York Times*, September 10, 2014, accessed 1.16.18, https://www.nytimes.com/2014/09/11/fashion/steve-jobs-apple-was-a-low-tech-parent.html.

project, and easy access to pornography—of iGen. And we need to think hard about how technology such as artificial intelligence disrupts the social fabric of our communities. Some are even wondering if the way we work today will be dramatically altered tomorrow. Self-driving cars, automatic checkout lanes, and other automated tasks are increasingly replacing real humans in real jobs.

But here is the danger. If all we do is furrow our brows about "kids these days," and pine for the days before smartphones when "everything was great and there was no sin," we are not only confusing the 1980s with Genesis 2, but we are missing an opportunity to press the Bible's compelling narrative of human dignity into the questions of the age. We cannot simply be the people standing athwart technology shouting, "No!" We need to have a positive story to tell about what it means to enjoy being a human made in God's image and redeemed by God's Son—and we need to have a positive message about the place of technology within the life we have been created to live.

This requires us to press in on the Bible's unique vision of humanity in a way that helps us hold our devices loosely and wrestle honestly with technology, so that we do not turn our back on our mandate to innovate in order to bless, but equally we take seriously the ways in which we are tempted to turn inward on ourselves in self-worship.

Therefore in some ways we will need to escalate our innovation and in some ways we will need to de-escalate our innovation. And it means we will need to think. All of us have a knee-jerk response to new technology: either "Oh yes, this is tremendous" or "Oh no, this is terrible." Neither should be embraced uncritically. This is especially important in the ways we choose to worship. We should not uncritically embrace what theologian Kevin Vanhoozer calls a "culture of spectacle," in which…

"the church's imagination is in danger of being captured by spectacular images that owe more to contemporary culture than to Christian faith ... I believe Scripture sets our imaginations free from the culture of spectacle so that we can see the world as it truly is: a good but fallen creation in which God's kingdom is advancing in mysterious and often quite unspectacular ways." [90]

ANALOG SUNDAYS

So perhaps the great antidote to the dehumanizing aspects of new technologies stares us in the face every Sunday. Our worship gatherings may be the most analog experience people have all week.

This may be why we might need to emphasize the embodied experience of corporate worship. Jesus told us that he is specially present "when two or three are gathered" in person, together as his body (Matthew 18 v 20). And in an individualistic society so easily disembodied and disconnected by social media, we possess in the local church the life-giving experience of biblical community. Church is where we experience real community, shoulder to shoulder, and not via FaceTime or Skype. There, we are known as we really are, challenged when we need it, forgiven, and spurred on. There, we don't need to put on a front or pretend. There we find a community of grace that we can rely on and contribute to, in place of a virtual community of performance and perfection that exhausts the soul.

Church as the gathered, embodied, physical presence of God's people has something to offer a world increasingly isolated in digital tribes. This is where we celebrate a meal together, physically raising the bread and the cup to our

---

90 "Discipleship in the Age of the Spectacle," Desiring God, April 2, 2016, accessed 1.16.18, http://www.desiringgod.org/articles/discipleship-in-the-age-of-the-spectacle.

lips in celebration of our status as God's redeemed image-bearers. It is where we hear God's word preached and shared together, as those made in his image to know him personally and look forward to seeing him face to face. It is where we sit down next to, and stand to sing with, and kneel to pray alongside those who are different than us in age, in viewpoint, or in personality type.

Think about the stunning simplicity of it all: the cure for our digital identity crisis and dehumanizing smartphone-worship might be to do the simple and analog act of going to church.

This ethos can then flow into the rest of our week, helping us form the spiritual habits we need to inform our everyday life and giving us a healthy grid through which we employ and enjoy our devices, and separate from and cease to rely upon our devices.

So the cure, then, from digital enslavement and to dignity-restoration, happens at an event wholly unlike the jaw-dropping spectacle I described at the beginning of this chapter. We find our dignity not in Cupertino, California, but in our local congregation.

The action doesn't need to take place in a sleek new amphitheater, but in any nondescript auditorium. The preacher is likely not as cool as Tim Cook and the media will send no one to cover your worship. But this is where, every Sunday, you reconnect with your humanity because you worship the God who formed you in his image in the midst of the community that he saved you to belong to. It's where the repeated rhythms of prayer, preaching, communion, and song form you for life in the world. The local church may not grip the news cycle, but it is where we learn to live as real people, producing technology, and enjoying and using technology, but not being dominated or shaped by it.

11. AGREE TO DISAGREE
PLURALISM, THE STATE, AND RELIGIOUS LIBERTY

"The right to follow our conscience lies at the center of human dignity and is the core of every other human right."

PAUL MARSHALL

They might be wrong, but I would die to protect their right to believe it."

If I heard this statement once while attending church as a child, I heard it a thousand times. My childhood pastor likely didn't know he was paraphrasing Voltaire, the eighteenth-century French philosopher, and, like most of what I heard in sermons, I didn't think much about this statement. But as an adult, spending my days working for an organization with religious liberty as its middle name, I often reflect back on what he said.

The right to believe is a vital aspect of what it means to be human. We are body, mind, and soul, with a rational ability that distinguishes us from the rest of creation. Part of being human is to be able to believe, and to be able to choose what we believe.

WHAT IS RELIGIOUS LIBERTY?

Perhaps the best definition of religious liberty is the one crafted by pastor and scholar Bart Barber:

> *"Religious liberty is the freedom to join or leave a religious movement without changing one's relationship, positively or negatively, with the state."* [91]

It is the provision of the civic space to discover, adopt, and make beliefs our own. Paul, often jailed for holding and promoting "wrong beliefs," nevertheless wrote to his protégé Timothy and asked him to pray for a government that would allow Christians to "lead a peaceful and quiet life, godly and dignified in every way" (1 Timothy 2 v 2). The Christians in first-century Rome never really saw that full freedom of religion and tragically, even once Constantine became emperor in the fourth century and the empire became a protector and then promoter of Christianity, Christians then didn't enshrine that freedom into law themselves.

In fact, the practice of religious liberty—something we often take for granted in Western democracies—is a fairly modern construct, and only exists in some parts of the world. According to the US State Department, 80% of the global population lives with restriction or hostility to religious practice.[92] So even as we engage in debates on this issue in open societies, we are doing it under an umbrella of protection we often don't fully appreciate.

---

91 Ed. Micah Fries and Keith Whitfield, *Islam and North America*, (B&H Academic, forthcoming).

92 Matthew Hawkins, "Religious Persecution a Sad Reality: State Department Releases 2016 IRF Report," ERLC, August 17, 2017, accessed 1.17.18, http://erlc.com/resource-library/articles/religious-persecution-a-sad-reality-state-department-releases-2016-irf-report.

IN WHOSE IMAGE?

The religious-liberty movement really finds its roots in the early separatist movements in England in the 1600s, culminating in the Toleration Act of 1689, which allowed non-Anglicans to worship freely. Religious liberty began to take root in America in the passing of the American Bill of Rights and the disestablishment of state churches. State-established religion was still very dominant in Massachusetts and Virginia and other states in the early colonial period, and free-church pastors were often kicked out of states, and church-discipline issues were often taken up by state legislatures. As a Baptist, I'm keenly aware of the work done by our forebears, like John Leland (whom our Washington, D.C. office is named after), and Roger Williams and Isaac Backus, in fighting for religious liberty and working with Thomas Jefferson and James Madison in enshrining it in the Bill of Rights—a document that today serves as a model for democracies all over the world.

So religious liberty as an idea has not been practiced throughout much of church history. In fact, church history mostly contains the bad fruit of some kind of relationship between church and state—an alliance that almost always ended up diluting the church's true witness and hurting the state.

But while religious liberty has not often been practiced, it has deep support in Scripture. Perhaps the clearest passage comes from Jesus himself in a well-known interaction with religious and civil authorities, when he was asked, both by those loyal to Rome and by their revolutionary foes, about paying tax to the Roman emperor. Both parties wished to score a victory against the other and to trap this rising trouble-maker into making a damaging gaffe. Jesus famously answered them by asking for a piece of currency, holding up the coin bearing Caesar's image and saying:

*Render to Caesar the things that are Caesar's, and to God
the things that are God's.*   MARK 12 V 17

Most of us just assume Jesus is telling us to pay our taxes
in full and on time, even if we would rather not. And yes,
Jesus is telling us to pay our taxes—but he's saying so
much more.

By asking the question, "Whose image is on this coin?"
Jesus is making a profound statement about what it means
to be human in a world ruled by God and a state ruled
by a human. He is saying, *Caesar is due your taxes because, as
someone granted temporary civil authority by me, Caesar has the
right to collect your taxes as he chooses.* Currency is part of how
a state functions. It bears its ruler's image. In this sense, it
belongs to him.

But, continues Jesus, you must "render ... to God the
things that are God's." And this is the real force of his
comment. Caesar does not have the right to demand everything from you. You were not made in the image of
Caesar. You were made in the image of the One who
sculpted Caesar, and you, from the dust of the ground;
and who breathed into Caesar, and you, the breath of life.
Therefore, your conscience does not belong to the state
but to God. "Caesar" has no right to demand you believe
what he chooses. God, your Creator, has authority over
your soul.

Or to put it another way, Jesus is telling the state that
it must protect, and not undermine, religious liberty. The
right to choose what to believe is a critical facet of being
made in God's image. It is intrinsic to human dignity.

In preparing this chapter, I sought out one of the foremost religious-liberty experts in the world: my friend and
colleague Andrew Walker. Andrew's PhD is in Christian
ethics, with a particular emphasis on religious liberty. I

asked him to expand on the connection between liberty and dignity. He explained it to me this way:

> *"One of the ways that humans find meaning and purpose is through rational inquiry. So we discover what is true because of the cognitive abilities God has placed in us. God puts in our hearts that we find meaning and purpose in him. If a person is not free to think authentically what they believe, and to then live that out, they are in no sense of the term free, at all. So, the very notion of freedom is connected to personhood and if we deny someone's freedom, we will end up denying his or her personhood."*

In this sense, to deny religious liberty or to coerce belief is to treat people as subhuman. It is to deny them their God-given capacity to think and rationalize and follow their conscience.

WHEN RIGHTS COLLIDE

But what about when it seems religious liberty and human rights seem to collide? This is a collision we see with increasing frequency in the West, and is often felt most acutely when the liberty of Christians and other religions comes into conflicts with the aims of LGBT activists. Christians who hold to a biblical sexual ethic are often expected to give up some of their right to practice and believe their convictions in order to accommodate the sexual revolution.

The state of California, for instance, sought to force religious institutions of higher education to disavow their convictions on sexual ethics, under threat of losing the ability to receive students who accept state-education grants. In Massachusetts, Gordon College nearly lost its accreditation because of its stated policy on sexual ethics. In Houston, pastors' sermons were subpoenaed by the mayor over a disagreement in a pending gay-rights ordinance. Vermont Senator Bernie Sanders berated Russell Vought, a nominee for deputy director of the US Office of Management and Budget, for a Facebook post in which he articulated the Christian doctrine of salvation by faith through Christ alone. In the UK, Tim Farron, leader of the "third party" of British national politics, the Liberal Democrats, stepped down because he had found committed Christianity to be incompatible with leading the Lib Dems, such was the battering he received from progressives in the media and in his own party (the irony of this occurring in a party bearing the name "Liberal" was lost on most). In 2017, the UK Government's then-Secretary of State for Education and Minister for Women and Equalities, Justine Greening, declared that "churches must be made to keep up with modern attitudes." The Speaker of the House of Commons issued a more direct threat, saying that the fight for gay rights won't end until it reaches the church sanctuary:

> *"We don't want to behave like it's all over, everything's been done and nothing remains, because that isn't true. I still feel we'll only have proper equal marriage when you can ... get married in a church if you want to do so, without having to fight the church for the equality that should be your right."* [93]

All these battles are, to quote the theologian and social commentator Albert Mohler, "the collision between erotic liberty and religious liberty." [94]

---

93 "Speaker John Bercow: We Don't Have Equal Marriage until It's in Churches," PinkNews, accessed 10.28.17, http://www.pinknews.co.uk/2017/07/18/speaker-john-bercow-we-dont-have-equal-marriage-until-its-in-churches/.

94 "Religious Liberty vs. Erotic Liberty—Religious Liberty Is Losing," Albert-Mohler.com, January 12, 2015, accessed 1.17.18, http://www.albertmohler.com/2015/01/12/religious-liberty-vs-erotic-liberty-religious-liberty-is-losing/.

You don't have to be a Christian to be troubled by this development, and to express doubt does not necessarily reveal you to be a right-wing reactionary alarmist. Gay-marriage advocate Douglas Laycock has expressed concern that perhaps the sexual revolution is mimicking the wrong lessons of the French Revolution and severing religion from liberty.[95]

Of course, this is all a far cry from the torture, imprisonment, and death faced by many in closed countries around the world, but these developments are still an encroachment on religious liberty and the ability to freely practice the Christian faith. And that should concern us, for as Karen Ellis reminds us, "Rarely does a nation move from freedom to oppression overnight."[96]

LIBERTY MUST LEAD TO MISSION

So, how should we respond? After all, didn't Jesus willingly lay down his rights and tell us to deny ourselves and follow him? Yes, he did. But he did also point out the injustice s of the way his trial proceedings were handled by the Jewish authorities (John 18 v 23). And Paul wasn't shy about asserting his rights as a Roman citizen (Acts 22 v 23-29). Further, as we have already mentioned, in writing to Timothy Paul essentially prayed for religious liberty:

> *I urge that supplications, prayers, intercessions, and thanksgivings be made for all people, for kings and all who are in high positions, that we may lead a peaceful and quiet life, godly and dignified in every way. This is good, and it is pleasing in the sight of God our Savior, who*

---

95 "Religious Liberty and the Culture Wars," accessed 11.10.17, http://illinoislaw-review.org/wp-content/ilr-content/articles/2014/3/Laycock.pdf.

96 "Are American Christians Really 'Persecuted'?" ChristianityToday.com, accessed 10.28.17, www.christianitytoday.com/ct/2016/september/are-us-christians-really-persecuted.html.

desires all people to be saved and to come to the knowledge of the truth. 1 TIMOTHY 2 V 1-4

Notice the way Paul connects religious liberty to gospel mission. Praying that Christians would be able to "lead a peaceful and quiet life" is not just an appeal for an easy life. Paul wants Christians—and everyone—to be able to follow what they believe in peace, so that God's people can live in a "godly and dignified" way, and so that "the truth" might be heard in the public square. Religious freedom is not an end in itself, but a means toward gospel proclamation, that "people [might be] saved."

In a sense, when we work for religious liberty—even if that is simply by using our vote in a way that promotes or defends it—we are not merely working for our own dignity to be recognized by the state, but for the dignity of our neighbors. Religious liberty, of course, is not our ultimate aim as Christians, but it's not unimportant either. Those who advocate in the public square this way are, in many ways, doing missionary work. The Christian lawyers and advocates who write opinions and take up cases are helping to clear the way for church planters and adoptive families and Christian relief organizations to do their work. If your church meets in a government or state-run school or in another public space, you do so under the umbrella of protection someone else fought to secure. If your ministry enjoys tax exemption or charitable status, or secures a building permit for your church expansion, it does do so thanks to the work of religious-liberty advocates who went before you. If your Christian institution is free to hire employees who adhere to your statement of faith, you have that freedom because someone else made sure this freedom was enshrined in the law.

This doesn't mean, of course, that the gospel's advance

is limited only to areas where religious liberty flourishes. The gospel has penetrated the most closed countries and most oppressive environments. The church will always endure, despite the tyrannies of dictators and despots. But religious liberty is a good thing, and it is one we are told to pray for, and work for, even as we remember that the church will not crumble without it. When Christians have the opportunity to shape the laws of the land, we should not shirk from our duties to help make possible what Paul prayed for (though never experienced himself): a public square that respects the conscience of our neighbors, created in the image of God.

WHAT RELIGIOUS LIBERTY ISN'T

At this point, it is important to underline what religious liberty is and what it isn't. Sometimes, particularly in America, religious liberty is confused with Christian privilege. This is where, frankly, many well-meaning American evangelicals have not adequately thought through the relationship between church and state. Some of our notions of working toward a "Christian nation" are at odds with religious liberty.

So, working to restore mandated Christian prayer in government schools is not working for religious liberty. That is the government favoring one religion over another. And, when we give the state the power to discern between religions and favor one, we are essentially granting them power over the conscience. We may enjoy this favor when Christians are in the majority, but we would not enjoy it if we were a minority faith. Imagine mandated Muslim prayers in schools, and you can see why state-sponsored religion is a bad idea.

Jesus implied, in his parable of the wheat and the tares, that it is his job to decide between believer and unbeliever

(Matthew 13 v 24-30, 36-43). I have much more confidence in the power of the kingdom of God to make that distinction than the power of the kingdoms of men. I pray my nation is led by wise Christians, but it is not the state's job to bind anyone's conscience. Remember, Jesus himself taught as he answered the question about Caesar's coin that only one conscience belongs to a leader, and that is their own. Furthermore, to demand that our nation be a "Christian" nation shows something of a lack of confidence in the power of the gospel to transform hearts and minds. We are saying, in effect, that we need the state to put its foot on the scale in our favor in order for us to live out the mission of God.

None of this means that we don't seek to make sure that what the Bible says is heard in our public debates. But it does mean that we should not demand specific privilege. Jesus said that the gospel does not need the power of the sword to accomplish his mission (John 18 v 36-37). He chastened his disciples when they wanted to coerce belief (Luke 9 v 51-56). Throughout history, churches that enjoyed the power of the state often had full sanctuaries, but were they full of genuine believers? Andrew Walker pointed out to me that coerced belief is not genuine belief:

> "I believe the gospel is true truth and it doesn't need cultural privilege or government force to be persuadable … You protect the image of God in someone when you recognize their true personhood. That person does have the ability to know right from wrong. That person with enough time could become a Christian. God has made us individuals in His image who are designed to seek after and pursue truth and meaning and purpose; so, when we allow that to happen freely and uncoercively, we are actually upholding the image of God in other people."

Laws are important reflections of our national character, but you cannot legislate conversion, nor pass any law that will change a person's heart. Barber says that one way of looking at religious liberty is that it ensures that governments "leave room for human repentance, for repentance is only genuine when it arises out of remorse and not out of coercion." British Baptist Thomas Helwys asserted back in the 16th century (when contending for religious liberty was something of a minority pursuit, liable to end in an early death):

> *"Men's religion to God is between God and themselves. The king shall not answer for it. Neither may the king be judge between God and man. Let them be heretics, Turks, Jews, or whatsoever, it appertains not to the earthly power to punish them in the least measure."* [97]

So rather than longing for Christian privilege, we should seek pluralism. At times, Christians wince at this idea because it seems to indicate we are losing something. But pluralism is not the same as relativism. Pluralism is not saying that all religions are equally true, but that all religions are to be debated freely and equally. In an essay for *The Student* the late Dallas Willard explained this well:

> *"Pluralism does not mean that everyone is equally right in what they think and do. It does not mean that we must agree with the views or adopt the practices of those of other persuasions. It does not mean that we must like those views or practices. It does not mean that we will not appropriately express our disagreement or dislike for other viewpoints.*
>
> *"Pluralism also does not mean that we will not try, in respectful ways, to change the views or practices of others,*

---

97 Thomas Helwys, *A Short Declaration of the Mystery of Iniquity* (this edition Mercer University Press, 1998), page 53.

by all appropriate means of persuasion, where we believe them to be mistaken. In fact, pluralism should, precisely, secure a social context in which full and free interchange of different views on life and reality can be conducted to the greatest advantage of all. Thin-skinned and narrow-minded people may not particularly enjoy a pluralistic society, but their discomfort is vastly outweighed by the benefits to all of open and free interchange of information and ideas. The Christian, perhaps more than anyone else, has reason to favor such interchange and be confident about its outcome." [98]

Since the ability to choose what to believe is part of what makes us human, we are not just to advocate for our own religious liberty, but for the religious liberty of faiths we believe are false. Sadly, many Christians have been unwilling to do this. Fear of terror has often caused Christians to fight against the religious freedom of our Muslim neighbors. Some Christian candidates have even lobbied for Muslim bans and religious tests for higher office. In a suburb of Nashville, where I live, a group of Christians lobbied to try to close down the building of a mosque. Sadly, this not only reflects poorly on our Christian witness; it again betrays a lack of confidence in the gospel. First-century Christians in the Roman Empire saw a multifaith society as an opportunity to share the gospel with those from very different creeds. In the twenty-first century, Christians are all too ready to see the same circumstance as an existential threat to be resisted at all costs.

To stand up for the religious liberty of religions that Christians believe to be false is not to affirm the validity of such religions, but to affirm the humanity of their adherents

---

98 "Being a Christian in a Pluralistic Society," *The Student*, 1922, accessed 5.15.18, download available at https://bit.ly/2Gi3B5E.

in a way that allows space for them to choose to believe the gospel. Walker says:

> *"It sounds strange to say this, but I want to uphold the integrity of the Muslim to believe what he believes sincerely because I believe he is made in the image of God, in order that I might be able to engage in serious conversation with him, persuasively and non-coercively, in order for him to come to the realization that he stands guilty before the holy God and is in need of a mediator."*

Working for and speaking up for the religious liberty of other religions is also an affirmation of the gospel's power. It reveals a confidence that Christianity can compete and win in the marketplace of ideas. It reflects a trust in the Holy Spirit's ability to draw men to Jesus. And it fulfills our duty to love our neighbors as ourselves by working for their liberty. If we truly believe that Christ is the reigning King, and is victorious over sin and death, and is coming back to judge the living and the dead, we should not fear the mosque or temple down the street but welcome the opportunity to show the love of Christ to our neighbors. Religious liberty either works for everyone or it works for no one.

LIMITS TO LIBERTY

This, of course, raises the question: does religious liberty have limits? Is religious liberty a blank check, justifying any kind of behavior? Where might we need to draw a line? This is, admittedly, a difficult question, but I think the answer, again, is rooted in human dignity.

Religious liberty cannot be a cover for religious practices that, even if sincerely held, infringe upon the dignity of others. Paul's desire was for a society that allows us to "live quiet and peaceable lives, dignified in every way." He urged Christians in Rome to, as much as was possible, "live peaceably with all" (Romans 12 v 18). There are deeply held religious practices that infringe the dignity of others. For instance, ancient Hindu practices demanded that widows be burned on the funeral pyre of their husbands. Some religions lead parents, by belief, to refuse life-saving treatment of their children. The Aztecs practiced human sacrifice. These are examples of religious practices that violate the dignity of image-bearers, prey on the vulnerable, and violate moral laws. Robert George says:

> *"Grave injustice can be committed by sincere people for the sake of religion. The presumption in favor of respecting liberty must be powerful and broad. But it is not unlimited."* [99]

When someone's religious freedom directly impacts the dignity of others, the government should step in, but only after careful consideration and by proving that there is a compelling human interest.

Now admittedly, this assumes some broad agreement on what is morally wrong—what is dignity-denying. This is part of the reason why the collision of sexual freedom and religious liberty is often so complex. LGBT advocates insist that affirmation of behavior is essential to human dignity, while Christians argue that dignity is not assigned to humanity based on human affirmation but by their Creator. This being the case, we can disapprove of behavior while still affirming the humanity and upholding the dignity of those with whom we disagree. A failure in society to come to some kind of agreement on what constitutes basic moral decency results in confusion. This is why, as we said in chapter 1, the Christian faith's robust view of

---

99 "What Is Religious Freedom?," *Public Discourse*, July 24, 2013, accessed 1.17.18, http://www.thepublicdiscourse.com/2013/07/10622/.

human dignity offers, perhaps, the most hope for societies that seek to carve out space for liberty.

These complex and nuanced intersections are why it is particularly important that we understand what is and what isn't religious liberty. We lose all credibility in areas where religious liberty is truly under threat if we only seek to protect our own liberty, or if we argue that the employee at Walmart saying "Happy Holidays" instead of "Merry Christmas" represents a violation of religious liberty, rather than just being annoying. (And, of course, demanding that that employee say "Happy Christmas" is to coerce behavior, and denies that person their full dignity.) We should be wise about the way we engage in these debates so we are fully prepared to defend religious liberty when it is actually imperiled.

SHAPING THE CLIMATE, ONE CONVERSATION AT A TIME

For most of us, life won't involve arguing cases before high courts or lecturing about religious liberty on college campuses—but that doesn't mean we don't all have a role to play in working toward a society that allows space for genuine belief.

We help shape the climate of our culture conversation by conversation. And we promote or diminish religious liberty in how we speak to and about others. We need to understand how to disagree with our neighbors in a way that honors their human dignity. This is what James is getting at when he warns us about the power of our tongues. Notice why he says our words about others matter:

> *With [our tongue] we bless our Lord and Father, and with it we curse people who are made in the likeness of God. From the same mouth come blessing and cursing.*
>
> JAMES 3 V 9-10

If we truly believe someone is created in the image of God, we will respect and love them, even in the midst of disputes over deeply-held views; and even as we try, like Paul, to persuade them to repent of their sins and idols and follow Jesus; and even if and when they disagree with us.

Religious liberty is written into law by law-makers, but a pluralistic public square begins first with the commitment of everyday believers to show the goodness of religious liberty in their lives.

Do we speak kindly of those with whom we disagree or do we spread untruths?

Do we work to get to know our neighbors who believe differently than we do?

Do we stand up for their dignity in conversations with others about them?

I'm particularly inspired by the words of the apostle Peter in these well-quoted verses:

> But in your hearts honor Christ the Lord as holy, always being prepared to make a defense to anyone who asks you for a reason for the hope that is in you; yet do it with gentleness and respect, having a good conscience, so that, when you are slandered, those who revile your good behavior in Christ may be put to shame.   1 PETER 3 V 15-16

Many of us have memorized the first part of Peter's words. We (rightly) endeavor to have a truthful gospel answer for every question raised in the culture. But we often ignore the part about "gentleness and respect." We can and should make arguments, engage in debates, and speak the truth—we must do it in a way that honors the dignity of those with whom we are arguing. Russell Moore says:

> "When we're dealing with people with whom we disagree, we're dealing with people who are reflecting back to us the

image of God, which means we see them as a mystery; we see them as a manifestation of the glory of God. "[100]

Civility is not a sign of weakness. It is a sign of strength, a reflection of our confidence in the power of the gospel to change hearts. Civility and courage are not enemies but friends.

We should fight for religious liberty, for ourselves and for our neighbors. We should make compelling arguments based on the human dignity of every person. And every one of us can model, by our lives and our speech, what respect and dignity look like.

I believe you to be wrong, but I will die for your right to believe it.

100 Bible Study Insider, "Religious Liberty and Human Dignity feat. Russell Moore," accessed 1.17.18, https://www.youtube.com/watch?v=O1r7vLW-JPZU.

12. A LAND BEYOND LEFT AND RIGHT
POLITICS

"The church is: a conspiracy of love for a dying world, a spy mission into enemy-occupied territory ruled by the powers of evil; a prophet from God with the greatest news the world has ever heard, the most life-changing and most revolutionary institution that has existed on earth."

PETER KREEFT

I'll never forget the first time I visited Washington, D.C. I was twelve and our family had decided to drive from the Chicago suburbs to our nation's capital. It was 1989.

From a young age, I was a rare and strange creature. While my friends were playing video games, I was (when not out doing plumbing with Dad) a political nerd, consuming our three Chicago newspapers almost daily, reading political journals, and engaging in lively debates with the family over dinner (whether they wanted those debates to take place or not!).

There was a moment in this trip to D.C. that planted the importance of public activism in my heart and mind. It was when I stood at the base of the Lincoln Memorial.

The image of the 16th President of the United States, who had given so much both to save the Union and defeat the evil institution of slavery, moved me. It is an emotional place for an American, I think—especially since it was also here that a century after the Civil War another American martyr, Martin Luther King Jr., stood and appealed both to Scripture and the American Declaration of Independence to remind millions of countrymen who had forgotten it or were ignoring it of the truth that all men are created equal.

A few years later, I would serve an internship in Springfield, the state capital of Illinois, where Lincoln began his public life, and where he engaged Senator Stephen Douglas in spirited debates about human dignity and public policy and the relationship between the two. The gilded halls where those two had traded arguments reminded me both of the perils and potential of political power.

For most of my life, in some form or another, I've been involved in public activism. Today I serve at the public policy agency for America's largest Protestant denomination. I've seen, up close, both the humbling power of Christian activism and the seamy underbelly of evangelical politics.

Today, even as I write this book in 2017, there is much renewed discussion, debate, and disagreement on the role of Christians in the public square, perhaps especially in the US, but also in other Western democracies. Politics seduces and it also repels.

This isn't a book about politics. This is a book about human dignity: about the image of God and how it should influence the way we think about the world. That is why I saved this chapter for the end. But if we come to a real understanding of human dignity, it will compel us, at some level, to engage with politics and the public square. There are, of course, different giftings and callings.

Some are called to a life of public service in elected or appointed office. Others are called to advocacy work, thought leadership, or journalism. For most Christians, though, politics is not an everyday calling. But none of us, I believe, can afford to be completely disengaged. Here are three reasons why.

1. POLITICS IS ABOUT STEWARDSHIP

We looked earlier at Jesus' words: "Render to Caesar the things that are Caesar's and to God the things that are God's" (Mark 12 v 17). This was not simply a clever push-back to two groups who were attempting to trap Jesus with their questions. He was making a statement about the authority of government and the authority of God.

Jesus is saying that, contrary to what the Romans believed, Caesar was not divine. He ruled only at the discretion of the divine. So Caesar was not to be worshiped. We are not created in Caesar's image, but in God's image. On the one hand, our leaders are due our respect, not necessarily because of their character or policies, but because of their offices. We should respect them (1 Peter 2 v 13-14, 17). But at the same time, we must not worship them. Only God owns the conscience. Juan Sanchez writes this about the age-old temptation to elevate our leaders to god-like status:

> "[The] practice of ruler-worship is not limited to the first century. Are we not worshiping a creature when we promote a particular leader (or party) as the answer to society's ills, the one who can inaugurate heaven on earth? Aren't we in danger of idolatry when we sacrifice time, money, and resources at the altar of a political party, but we won't sacrifice time, money, and resources to advance the gospel to the ends of the earth? And what does it say about us when we speak of a mere human as an evil

*power that rivals God, as though the wrong election result
might well bring hell on earth?"*[101]

So Caesar is not divine, but he is not irrelevant either.
We are tempted to make too much of our government
or system of rule—but we must not make too little of it
either.

Paul teaches us that all authority and power is "institut-
ed by God" as "God's servant for your good" (Romans 13
v 1, 4). In a representative democracy, this not only means
that the leaders will be held accountable to God for the
God-given power they possess; it also means that those
who have the responsibility of electing their leaders, of
influencing public policy, and of influencing the debate in
the public square will also be held accountable.

In other words, Jesus' words and Paul's words remind us
that in many ways, in a representative republic, the people
themselves function in certain ways as Caesar.

Our freedoms—the opportunity to vote, to shape policy,
to influence the public debate—are a gift and a stewardship from God. To completely disengage is an abdication
of this stewardship. In the parable of the talents, remember, it was the one who buried his treasure who was judged
most harshly. Those of us who live in societies where citizenship means a share of power should think wisely about
the ways we invest this gift. It is not good enough to say
that we are not interested in politics or don't think politicians are worthy of our time or our prayers, any more than
it is good enough to locate all our hopes and dreams (even
at the expense of compromising our integrity) in a particular platform or leader.

---

101 "What Now? Three Principles for Living as Christians under President
Trump," The Good Book Blog, accessed 11.28.17, https://www.thegoodbook.
com/blog/news/2016/11/09/three-principles-president-trump/. See also his
1 Peter For You (The Good Book Company, 2016), pages 100-101.

2. POLITICS IS ABOUT LOVING YOUR NEIGHBOR

There are, famously, two commandments that sum up the whole of God's law. Jesus commands us to "love the Lord your God with all your heart and with all your soul and with all your mind," and to "love your neighbor as yourself" (Matthew 22 v 37, 39). If we would do the first, we must do the second. Christian witness is not simply about vertical piety, but horizontal love.

There are many ways we show love for our neighbors. We serve them by looking out for their needs, respecting their property, and caring for them in a crisis. Mostly we love our neighbor by declaring to them the good news of the gospel: that in Christ they can be reconciled to the Creator who made them in his image.

But our neighbor-love can't stop there. We have to ask ourselves: can we adequately and fully love our neighbors if we are ignoring the opportunity to shape the social structures that affect them and the government that will rule over them?

Can we say that we love our unborn neighbors if we have an opportunity to speak out for their lives, but don't?

Can we say that we love our neighbors who are living below the poverty line if we have an opportunity to speak out for their welfare, but don't?

Can we say that we love our trafficked and enslaved neighbors if we don't work for their freedom?

Can we say that we love our immigrant neighbors if we are silent as they are mistreated?

We can't.

It is common today to hear Christians argue for a retreat from the "culture wars." To that, I want to ask, "Which ones?" Every time Christians apply the gospel to their communities, they are, at some level, engaged in "culture warring." They are bringing the kingdom of Christ to bear on this fallen world—a world that has been corrupted by the enemy. Kingdom ethics are rubbing up against fallen priorities. It's a battle of light against darkness.

There are, of course, unnecessary partisan and tribal skirmishes that are more about scoring points against "the other side" than about principles. When we defend "our candidates," even when they are wrong or untrustworthy or take cheap shots at "the other side," we do damage to Christian witness and alienate those God has called us to love. Some issues are matters of principle, but sometimes we're fighting hard and taking casualties about things that are not worth it. You and I may have a different vision for what the top marginal tax rate should be, but I can't locate my theory in Scripture and neither can you, and we should be willing to disagree agreeably without besmirching each other's characters or breaking friendship with each other.

Still, we must realize that every time we worship Jesus, every time we go to church, every time we change how we live based on what we've heard or read in God's word, every time we sing a Christian song or read a Christian book, we are engaging in a culture war. When we live our lives for Christ, we are saying, like the apostles in the first century, "There is another King and another kingdom. No leader in this world is the greatest king; no creed from this world is ultimate truth."

A complete culture-war timeout would mean no Christians fighting human trafficking, no Christians advocating for racial justice, no Christians pointing to the unborn and declaring their personhood.

So yes, we need to move beyond the tired old "culture war" trope. But also yes, there is a culture war that we are called to continue to fight.

After all, a gospel so safe that it experiences no friction with prevailing norms and worldviews is a half-gospel that stays cloistered within the four walls of the church, failing to move God's people to love their neighbors, to care about human flourishing, or to embody the ethics of the kingdom. It is not the triumphant, world-altering good news Jesus delivered. To abandon our public role is to tell our neighbors that we don't see their humanity and that we prize our own safety instead of their welfare.

The prophet Jeremiah told the humiliated and exiled people of God living in the pagan culture of Babylon that their role was not to huddle together and wait for deliverance, but to build and plant, create and shape. They were to "seek the welfare of the city" (Jeremiah 29 v 7). Today, the people of God are similarly called to live on mission in the cities where they have been placed. We are called to love our cities and our communities because cities and communities are made up of image-bearers whom God loves. We do this knowing that we'll never create a utopia; but we can give glimpses of heaven, pockets of hope in a world of hopelessness. And so politics is neighbor-love writ large.

3. POLITICS IS ABOUT SPEAKING TO CONSCIENCES

When we use our freedom to speak up for the vulnerable, to point to a kingdom ethic, and to work for good government and good leadership, we are speaking to consciences that can be worked in and formed by the Spirit of God. When we speak a gospel word—a prophetic word—to the culture, we aim that some who hear us will have their heads and their hearts stirred. Some who most vociferously oppose us may one day be transformed by the Spirit of God and become our brothers and sisters in Christ. We speak to the law written on the hearts of men (Romans 2 v 15). Paul says that it is part of the mission of every Christian to engage with "arguments and every opinion against the knowledge of

God" (2 Corinthians 10 v 5). The Spirit of God is powerful enough to take our feeble arguments and use them to convict the hearts of those who hear and overhear. And even when he does not choose to use our witness in this way, we are still standing up and saying to those around us, with gentleness and respect, that there is another way, a better way, a more dignified way.

A POLITICS OF DIGNITY (AND WITH DIGNITY)

Politics is necessary—but is there a way to do politics that transcends the zero-sum, soul-crushing, gospel-denying way that it is often conducted? In the last few years, I've become increasingly disenchanted with both the left and the right in my country. We are, it seems, becoming increasingly tribal, defending the worst kind of behavior in our own candidates while attacking the low character of candidates in the other party. Even Christians have succumbed to the moral relativism of the age, excusing immoral and disgusting behavior because it is "their guy" or "their girl."

What's more, it seems that if you care about human dignity, there really is no home for you. Conservatives, rightly, champion the lives of the unborn, but seem indifferent or even antagonistic toward the dignity of the immigrant or the refugee. Liberals rightly champion the dignity of immigrants and refugees, but can't seem to see the personhood of the unborn. It is a fresh reminder that as sojourners and exiles (1 Peter 2 v 11), we will never be fully at home in any earthly political movement or party. But maybe that is exactly the way God intended it to be. Scott Sauls, the pastor and author, put it well when he tweeted that because he follows Jesus he is "too conservative for liberals, and too liberal for conservatives."

There is a better way. Rather than being defined by our tribes (whether conservative or liberal or libertarian or socialist or independent or "a plague on all your houses"), imagine instead politics not as the ultimate end, but as a way of helping to advocate for the human dignity of those whose voices have been diminished. Imagine a movement that looks around and sees those who we've been conditioned to not see. Imagine a political system where we hold loosely to our tribes, but hold firmly to our broken-heartedness about the vulnerable, our theology of human dignity, our hope in the power of the Spirit to change people, systems, and nations, and our pursuit of the true, and good, and beautiful.

That would be a politics worth having.

THE POLITICS OF THE JERICHO ROAD

Every week, it seems, some cheeky commentator is out with a book elucidating the "politics of Jesus," but if you really want to see how Jesus sees power, you need look no further than the well-told story of the Good Samaritan in Luke 10. Today this story inspires—we name hospitals and charities and churches after the good Samaritan—but in Jesus' day there was no such thing, in the mind of a religious Jew, as a good Samaritan. They were half-breeds, outcasts, and religiously heterodox.

But to a religious establishment bent on finding loopholes in God's command to "love your neighbor as yourself," Jesus told this yarn about an injured man on a dangerous roadway near Jericho. Two people, with power and agency, passed by this man. The Levite and priest both were religious. Both should have stopped and helped. Both, however, didn't see the injured man because they had been conditioned to not see the vulnerable or because they had become convinced that their religious activity was more important than acting for their neighbor. Injured people on the roadside cannot help you secure that next position or contract or speaking gig. They are just... there. Broken people cannot make your life more comfortable or easy. They are costly and expensive and time-consuming.

But a Samaritan(!) of all people stopped, and used his money, his connections, and his agency to help rescue and heal this injured man. A Samaritan is the hero of the story. And Jesus is telling us here about what he calls for and prizes in the citizens of his kingdom. He is not pleased when we look for loopholes and walk on by. He is pleased when we see the vulnerable and cross the road and get involved and make a difference.

What if our public engagement of issues, the way we vote, the people on whose behalf we speak, the way we talk, and the way we listen were shaped less by tribal loyalties and more by the way of Jesus? What if we held firmly to orthodoxy, but held loosely our opinions about complex political issues, so that when we encounter someone at church or on Facebook who thinks differently we are able to listen with ears to hear? This doesn't mean that we won't have to make difficult voting decisions or that we will all agree on the best public policies. What it does mean, however, is that the axis around which we shape our politics will be shaped by a desire to use our power and our platforms to advocate on behalf of those who may have no voice.

IMAGINE...

Imagine a new human-dignity movement, which transcends and ignores and gets beyond existing tribal loyalties.

Seeing people as God sees them—created in his image—means we will often have to refuse to prioritize one interest group above another. It means we will have to stop compartmentalizing our views of human dignity. I've seen younger evangelicals who are rightly, wonderfully drawn to speak out on behalf of refugees and victims of human trafficking and the poor, but who are also tempted to silence on behalf of the unborn because this would put them in agreement with more conservative older generations whom they perceive as the enemy. And I've seen older generations of evangelicals, rightly concerned about the dignity of unborn human life, hesitant to speak out on issues of race and poverty because it might put them at odds with their ideological allies.

I see one cause pitted against another, as if human dignity is a zero-sum game.

We need to stop choosing. We need to start caring about dignity wherever it is undermined and assaulted.

This doesn't mean there won't be differing callings, or that we won't feel compelled to advocate for one particular area where humans are not being treated with dignity. But we should commit to learning about and sympathizing with all aspects of human dignity, and learn to speak in language and care about issues that reach beyond the amen chorus of our own constituencies.

A genuine Jesus-follower realizes that he has no permanent home in any one tribe. My friend Michael Wear, who worked in the Office of Faith-Based Initiatives for President Barack Obama, wrote candidly about his time in the White House and the way politics often serrates the edges of our souls:

> *"The crisis for Christians is not that we are politically homeless, but that we ever thought we could be at home in politics at all."* [102]

We must resist letting our politics shape our faith instead of our faith shaping our politics. This will take great courage. It will mean being criticized, at times, for being too conservative and being criticized, at times, for being too liberal. But

---

102 "No Political Home," *WORLD Magazine*, accessed 6.9.17, https://world.wng. org/2017/05/no_political_home.

a public witness that never crosses the aisle or that is galvanized by fear of the other party is not a public witness that loves our neighbors well. If we are going to stand alongside the people our King most delighted in visiting—the lowly, the meek, the vulnerable—we cannot let our worldly alliances dictate our words and silences, our action and inaction.

We need a fully-orbed pro-life vision that enters the public square and speaks up for human dignity wherever it is compromised, whether in the womb, on the streets of Baltimore, Cleveland and New York, at the nursing home, in the halls of power, or at the border. We are redeemed image-bearers, who have been recreated by Christ in the gospel, and we are now tasked with fighting for human dignity all around us.

> *[God] has told you, O man, what is good; and what does the*
> *LORD require of you but to do justice, and to love kindness,*
> *and to walk humbly with your God?* MICAH 6 V 8

And do not think that things are different now that Jesus has come, that our task has now focused only on proclaiming the gospel. The following words are from a New Testament epistle, not an Old Testament prophet:

> *Religion that is pure and undefiled before God the Father*
> *is this: to visit orphans and widows in their affliction, and*
> *to keep oneself unstained from the world.* JAMES 1 V 27

BEYOND POLITICS

And yet, as much as I am urging Christians to enlist in the fight to contend for human dignity in the public square, I'm urging us to remember that politics isn't everything; in fact, that it is but a small part of what it means to live on mission for God in this world. For every argument we make online or in the office of a public official, there are hundreds of interactions in our daily lives that test whether we really think every person is made in God's image. Human dignity is more than a platform; it's a way of life.

I can loudly contend for the vulnerable on my Twitter account, but if I'm a passive, uninvolved father, I really don't believe what I say I believe about human dignity. I can write letters to my congressman about an issue of concern, but if I'm treating my colleagues at work with little regard, I am, as Paul says, but a "clanging cymbal" (1 Corinthians 13 v 1). I can be right in every way, and at the same time love no one. I can win the argument, and at the same time sear my conscience and sap my soul.

After all, if we are on the side of the Victor, we should be joyful warriors, not rage-filled emulators of our enemy (1 Peter 5 v 8). Our ideological opponents are not avatars to be crushed, but people. Real people. Politics matters, but not as much as we often think it does. And it's certainly not worth the integrity of our public witness.

The most important thing happening in the world is what happens when we gather together in community in worship of the risen Christ. Standing and declaring through song, through prayer, in the reading and preaching of the word—this holds the power to change communities and nations. When we gather, Jesus is there, in our midst. Platforms come and go. Political fortunes rise and fall. But the gospel will continue to move in the hearts of God's people, as it has for two thousand years.

So we lend our voices to important issues, write our public officials, and roll up our sleeves in working to help our communities flourish, remembering that the best work is not happening on our television sets or in marble halls of power or via hashtags. It is happening, first, in big and small congregations around the world. Some meet in glorious cathedrals. Others meet in homes in secret for fear of their lives. All are celebrating and declaring this world-changing gospel that tells the world that humans are not disposable, but have dignity, regardless of their utility.

We have too often allowed our politics to tear at the unity we have in Christ. Those of us who are more engaged in activism than others need, at times, to reflect on the way we have done politics. Every election season provides fresh temptations to endorse candidates in a way that alienates us from our brothers and sisters in Christ and from our neighbors in the world. Frankly, many of us need to repent of the things we've said on social media, the leaders we've anointed as "God's man" or "God's woman," and the way we are tempted to twist the gospel to score cheap points for our side.

Before we are activists, we are worshipers. But equally, if we are truly worshipers, we will be activists; because we worship a great God, and it is his image that we see in every person— for *every* person has God-given dignity, no matter their utility.

A person's a person, no matter how small.

OUTRO:
LEARNING FROM THE ZONG
WHAT WILL BE OUR LEGACY?

"We must confront the world now with an ethics to make it tremble, and with a dynamic to give it hope."

CARL F.H. HENRY

In 1781 the British vessel, the Zong, ran out of drinkable water as it made its way from Africa to Jamaica. This was due to poor planning and nautical errors on the part of the captain and crew. The ship, originally built by the Dutch and ironically first named the Zorg (meaning "Care"), carried 442 African slaves.

133 slaves were thrown overboard, including 54 women and children.

By the time the ship reached Jamaica, only 208 Africans had survived.

The Zong Massacre, as it became known, came to light when back in England the ship's owners tried to cash in on their insurance policy, since slaves were considered property. The insurance company disputed the claim, but lost.

One effect of the resulting court case was to catalyze an emerging abolitionist movement, especially among

London Quakers. Soon after, those Quakers sent Thomas Clarkson—a young man who had recently won an essay-writing prize at Cambridge University in which he argued that slavery was morally wrong—to Bristol, a city built on the profits of the slave trade. They tasked him with researching the slave trade and Bristol people's views of it. Clarkson was an evangelical who would become one of the foremost opponents of the slave trade. But this was his first exposure to people who knew about it, and in some cases had profited from it.

In his diary, he wrote of his trip to Bristol:

> *"In my first movements about the city I found that people talked very openly on the subject of the slave trade. They seem to be well acquainted with the various circumstances belonging to it. There were facts, in short, in everybody's mouth concerning it and everybody seemed to execrate it, though no one thought of its abolition."*

No one thought of its abolition. Today, those words are hard for us to fathom, because British slave-trading is a thing of the past. Many of us have read books or watched films about William Wilberforce, Clarkson's friend, who came to lead the anti-slave-trade movement.

But there was a time, in the not-so-distant past, when the end of the slave trade seemed impossible.

Today when we consider the slave trade, we wonder how people could have thought it was OK. But the insight from Clarkson's diary is this: they did not think it was OK. "Everybody seemed to execrate [that is, to feel or express great loathing for] it."

They knew about it.

They didn't agree with it.

They couldn't imagine that the status quo could be changed.

They didn't do anything about it.

Lord Mansfield, the judge in the Zong trial, said something very similar: that the jury in the first trial "had no doubt (though it shocks one very much) that the Case of Slaves was the same as if Horses had been thrown overboard." There were too many economic, political, and social reasons for not doing anything.

This is always the case, and therefore this is always the risk. Opposing assaults on human dignity today brings us into conflict with economic and political interests, and social norms and pressures. Speak against abortion, for instance, and you'll be unwelcome in some places in society. Speak against racial injustice, and you'll be unwelcome in just as many places. Lift your finger against oppression and you'll immediately find a tribe of people opposed to you, sometimes including those close by. And so the risk is that we know about the ways human dignity is undermined. We don't agree with it. We can't imagine it can change.

And so we do nothing about it.

But we must ask ourselves the question: what will the church, in this period of human history, be remembered for? Will we be the people that, because of our faith in the risen Christ, point to the most vulnerable and stand up to declare: "There is a person here, worthy of dignity." Or will we be guilty of knowing that all humans are made in God's image, and knowing that all humans have innate and inalienable dignity, and knowing the ways in which the systems and laws of our society propagate injustices… and then not doing anything about it?

Are we content merely to be shocked as we scroll down our timelines and watch our news channels, even to "execrate it," and then do… nothing?

Or will we embrace and pursue a quiet activism? An activism that, yes, marches and writes and engages on social media, but that also and primarily goes about investing our money, donating our time, opening our homes, and sacrificing our ease to love our neighbors—all our neighbors? Will we pray and work so that in any and every area where human dignity is threatened and trampled, we or those who follow on from us may one day write what Clarkson did when the slave trade was abolished throughout the British Empire:

> *"Thus ended one of the most glorious contests, after a continuance for twenty years, of any ever carried on in any age or country. A contest, not of brutal violence, but of reason. A contest between those, who felt deeply for the happiness and the honor of their fellow-creatures, and those, who, through vicious custom and the impulse of avarice, had trampled under-foot the sacred rights of their nature, and had even attempted to efface all title to the divine image from their minds."* [103]

I want to suggest that the fight for human dignity is the cause of our generation. And you and I are the people whom God is calling. Regardless of what your gifting is, or where he places you, or what position you are in, or what role you play—fight for humanity. And may it be that when the last chapter of our generation is written—when the history is told of what we did in our time on this earth—it will be said that of all people, it was those Christians—those people who believed in a crucified, buried, and risen Savior—who uniquely stood up for the human dignity of those who could not speak up for themselves.

Some of us may be called—right now—to take a very public stand, to engage in defending dignity in high-

103 *The History of the Rise, Progress, and Accomplishment of the Abolition of the African Slave Trade by the British Parliament* (first published 1808; Qontro Classic Books, 2010).

profile ways. Perhaps we are called to fight mainly in one particular part of the cause. Every generation needs its Wilberforce and its Clarkson, its Shaftesbury, Fry, Lincoln, and MLK.

But we are not all called to high-profile activism. Most of us are all called to quiet activism. An activism that looks at everybody and sees the dignity of an image-bearer of our Creator... and then acts accordingly. None of us are called to affirm that a person's a person, no matter how small—and then do nothing. Let our legacy not be a generation who let go of our Christian beliefs; or a generation who held on to our Christian beliefs but said nothing about them, and did nothing about them; or a generation who only spoke out about one dignity-diminishing failure of our society, while ignoring the others.

Let us lament injustice and long for God's coming kingdom.

Let us be quiet activists.

Let us be the people of God.

And let us change our world, one life, one moment, one act of quiet activism at a time.

ACKNOWLEDGMENTS

It takes a village to write a book and this book is no different. This is where I'd like to offer some gratitude for those who helped make it possible. First, to the publisher, The Good Book Company: thank you for not only understanding this idea of human dignity but being so enthusiastic about the possibility of this book. Brad Byrd, Carl Laferton, and the rest of your team: thank you. I'm also indebted to my literary agent, Erik Wolgemuth of Wolgemuth and Associates: thank you for shepherding this process through.

To the interns who helped me organize my research, catalog my sources, and were nimble enough to answer emails like, "I think Tim Keller said this somewhere. Can you find it?" Eric Wolffe, Conrad Close, Lauren Konkol, and Alex Ward: you were amazing and helpful. To my communications team: thank you for both allowing me space to write this book and for being such an awesome group of people to lead. Especially Marie, for making my crazy schedule work so well.

To my colleagues Andrew Walker, Trillia Newbell, and Jason Thacker: thank you for reading some of my chapters and giving me critical, important, insightful feedback. To my boss: Phillip Bethancourt, thanks for enthusiastically embracing this book idea and giving me space and time to write it.

To my friends Bruce Ashford and Trevin Wax, who read through some chapters and gave me some great direction on the idea of human dignity. To Carl Laferton (yes, he gets two mentions—please don't edit) who, more than any book editor I've ever had, worked hand in hand with me to shape this book. When people say "working with an editor," this is what they mean.

Finally, I want to thank my dear wife of fifteen years, Angela. Not only has she endured life with me for nearly a decade and a half, but she has pushed me to write, especially in those lonely moments when I've wanted to give up—that inevitable season of doubt and despair that occurs every single time I write a book. Not only did she provide encouragement; she managed our home during those long days when I'd be hunkered down in front of my laptop. Angela, Daniel, Emma, and Lily: Daddy is free now! And Angela, you are awesome.

the good book
C O M P A N Y

BIBLICAL | RELEVANT | ACCESSIBLE

At The Good Book Company, we are dedicated to helping Christians and local churches grow. We believe that God's growth process always starts with hearing clearly what he has said to us through his timeless word—the Bible.

Ever since we opened our doors in 1991, we have been striving to produce resources that honour God in the way the Bible is used. We have grown to become an international provider of user-friendly resources to the Christian community, with believers of all backgrounds and denominations using our Bible studies, books, evangelistic resources, DVD-based courses and training events.

We want to equip ordinary Christians to live for Christ day by day, and churches to grow in their knowledge of God, their love for one another, and the effectiveness of their outreach.

Call us for a discussion of your needs or visit one of our local websites for more information on the resources and services we provide.

Your friends at The Good Book Company

NORTH AMERICA		thegoodbook.com	 866 244 2165
UK & EUROPE		thegoodbook.co.uk	0333 123 0880
AUSTRALIA		thegoodbook.com.au	(02) 9564 3555
NEW ZEALAND		thegoodbook.co.nz	(+64) 3 343 2463

 WWW.CHRISTIANITYEXPLORED.ORG
Our partner site is a great place for those exploring the Christian faith, with a clear explanation of the good news, powerful testimonies and answers to difficult questions.